EATING
AND
ISSUES

Jay Vaughan and Alan Burnell
with Jo Jackson and Daniel Swanson

Published by
CoramBAAF Adoption and Fostering Academy
41 Brunswick Square
London WC1N 1AZ
www.corambaaf.org.uk

Coram Academy Limited, registered as a company limited by
guarantee in England and Wales number 9697712, part of the
Coram group, charity number 312278

Section I © Jay Vaughan and Alan Burnell 2021
Section II © individual authors, 2021

British Library Cataloguing in Publication Data
A catalogue record for this book is available from the British Library

ISBN 978 1 913384 05 0

Project management by Jo Francis, Publications, CoramBAAF
Photograph on cover from www.istockphoto.com
Designed and typeset by Fravashi Aga
Printed in Great Britain by the Lavenham Press
Trade distribution by Turnaround Publisher Services, Unit 3,
Olympia Trading Estate, Coburg Road, London N22 6TZ

All rights reserved. Apart from any fair dealing for the purposes of
research or private study, or criticism or review, as permitted under
the Copyright, Designs and Patents Act 1988, this publication may
not be reproduced, stored in a retrieval system, or transmitted in
any form or by any means, without the prior written permission of
the publishers.

The moral rights of the authors have been asserted in accordance
with the Copyright, Designs and Patents Act 1988.

 For the latest news on CoramBAAF titles and special offers, sign up
to our free publications bulletin at https://corambaaf.org.uk/subscribe.

Contents

Looking behind the label…
Introduction ix

SECTION I
UNDERSTANDING EATING AND FOOD ISSUES 1

1 Normal development of eating and good
   nutrition for children 3
2 The impact of trauma on eating and nutrition 14
3 A neuro-physiological understanding of
   eating and nutrition 20
4 A step-by-step approach to eating and food difficulties 27
5 Frequently asked questions 46
   Conclusion 58

SECTION II
PARENTING CHILDREN AFFECTED BY EATING AND FOOD ISSUES 61

A window on Harry's world 63
Jo Jackson

A pocketful of mashed potatoes 83
Daniel Swanson

References 106
Glossary 112
Useful organisations 117

Notes about the authors

Alan Burnell OBE (for services to adopted children) is a registered social worker who qualified at Goldsmith's College London and progressed to an Advanced Diploma in working with children and families. He has been a local authority social worker and team manager of a fostering and adoption service. He left to become one of the initial counselling team at the Post Adoption Centre in London, where he eventually became director. In 1998, Alan was one of the founding members of Family Futures and for 20 years, until his retirement in 2019, he was Registered Manager of the agency.

Alan helped to pioneer post-adoption services for children and their adoptive families and has been at the forefront of integrating neuro-scientific research and theory into family placement practice in the UK. In 2015, he received a lifetime achievement award for his work in adoption.

Alan has contributed to many articles and books. He has also been involved in training parents and professionals involved in adoption, fostering and kinship care.

Jay Vaughan MA is a State Registered Dramatherapist, a Certified Dyadic Developmental Psychotherapist (DDP), a Theraplay Therapist and trainer, as well as a Somatic Experience Practitioner. Jay is Registered Manager and CEO of Family Futures, a voluntary adoption agency based in London. Jay has contributed to many articles and books and continues to consult and train around the UK on behalf of Family Futures, and still carries out some direct work with families and children.

Family Futures, founded in 1988, specialises in the assessment and treatment of traumatised children placed in foster families, adoptive families, special guardianship families or in kinship care. Family Futures offers an assessment and treatment programme called Neuro-Physiological Psychotherapy, which integrates Somatic Experience, Theraplay and DDP as part of the assessment and treatment approach.

Jo Jackson came out of a long-term relationship at the age of 40. The search for the other parent of her children having come to nothing, she realised that it was time to strike out on her own. She was determined to have her family and then later, to change career. After going through the assessment process with two different agencies, she finally found herself in the right place to meet "Harry" (a pseudonym) at the age of 45. Nearly ten years later, she hopes that she's learned enough from Harry to be able to carve out a career for herself in adoption.

Daniel Swanson is a pseudonym, as are the other names in his story. Daniel is an American-born 30-something "creative" who lives with his husband and their wonderful adopted son. Two years ago, the Swansons moved to the countryside where they found space and freedom without the many distractions of the city. They may or may not have two dogs, a cat, five chickens and two canaries when this book is published. Daniel enjoys reading, baking and fossil hunting with his son, gardening, long walks through dragon-infested forests, and any form of creative expression.

The series editor
Hedi Argent is an established author and editor. Her books cover a wide range of placement topics. She has written several guides and story books for young children.

Acknowledgements
Thank you to all the team at Family Futures as we would not have learned all we have learned without them. A special thank you to all the families we have worked with over the years from whom we have also learned so much.

Thank you particularly to Family Futures assistant psychologist Dixie Noruschat for her literature review and to Morag Best, Sensory Integration Therapist, for her sensory integration information and strategies, and focus on the complexity of eating.

We are grateful to Dr Jeanne Magagna, Ellie Johnson (CoramBAAF) and Sarah Borthwick for reading and commenting on the final draft of this book.

Looking behind the label...

Jack has mild learning difficulties and displays some characteristics of ADHD and it is uncertain whether this will increase...

Beth and Mary both have a diagnosis of global developmental delay...

Abigail's birth mother has a history of substance abuse. There is no clear evidence that Abigail was prenatally exposed to drugs but her new family will have to accept developmental uncertainty...

Jade has some literacy and numeracy difficulties, but has made some improvement with the support of a learning mentor...

Prospective adopters and carers are often faced with the prospect of having to decide whether they can care for a child with a health need or condition they know little about and have no direct experience of. No easy task...

Will Jack's learning difficulties become more severe?
Will Beth and Mary be able to catch up?
When will it be clear whether or not Abigail has been affected by parental substance misuse?
And will Jade need a learning mentor throughout her school life?

It can be difficult to know where to turn for reliable information. What lies behind the diagnoses and "labels" that many looked after children bring with them? And what will it be like to live with them? How will they benefit from family life?

Parenting Matters is a unique series, "inspired" by the terms used – and the need to "decode" them – in profiles of children needing new permanent families. Each title provides expert knowledge about a particular condition, coupled with facts, figures and guidance presented in a straightforward and accessible style. Each book also describes what it is like to parent an affected child, with either case studies or adopters and foster carers "telling it like it is", sharing their parenting experiences, and offering useful advice. This combination of expert information and first-hand experiences will help readers to gain understanding, and to make informed decisions.

Titles in the series deal with a wide range of conditions and steer readers to where they can find more information. They offer a sound introduction to the topic under consideration and provide a glimpse of what it would be like to live with an affected child. Most importantly, this series looks behind the label and gives families the confidence to look more closely at a child whom they otherwise might have passed by.

Keep up with all our new books as they are published by signing up to our free publications bulletin at: https://corambaaf.org.uk/subscribe.

Titles in this series include:

- *Parenting a Child with Attention Deficit Hyperactivity Disorder*
- *Parenting a Child with Dyslexia*
- *Parenting a Child with Mental Health Issues*
- *Parenting a Child affected by Parental Substance Misuse*
- *Parenting a Child with Emotional and Behavioural Difficulties*
- *Parenting a Child with Autism Spectrum Disorder*
- *Parenting a Child with Developmental Delay*
- *Parenting a Child with, or at risk of, Genetic Disorders*
- *Parenting a Child affected by Domestic Violence*
- *Parenting a Child affected by Sexual Abuse*
- *Parenting a Child who has experienced Trauma*
- *Parenting a Child with Toileting Issues*
- *Parenting a Child with Sleep Issues*

Introduction

Why are eating and food so important for healthy functioning?

Food tends to be an emotive and powerful issue, which brings with it a vast array of emotions!

If you ask any parent of a new infant what they struggled with most in the early days of parenting, one of the answers is whether to breast feed or to bottle feed; after four to six months, it is how to wean their child from a milk-based diet to solid food. Later, the challenge for most parents is how to ensure that their children or adolescents are eating a healthy diet. These are normal challenges for any parent. And yet, when we place children in new families, it is not necessarily anticipated that food and eating will present problems.

There are four pillars of parenting infants and children:

- sleep;
- food;
- toileting;
- attachment.

This book will explore issues around food and eating, because they are often problematic for a number of reasons for children who are, or have been, in care. Food and eating are of great importance as key indicators of health. If children are not eating well, then it is almost impossible for the other three pillars of parenting – sleep, attachment and toileting – to be secure. Food and eating difficulties can be extremely challenging for the child as well as for the parent or carer, and can lead to conflict and distress.

The eating experience and food are complex areas in child development. Food is necessary for:

- complex neuro-physiological motor skill development required for eating;
- sustenance for healthy development, including the development of the brain and nervous system;
- an opportunity for relational interaction with parents and primary caregivers, which means that it is therefore one of the foundations for secure attachments.

This book is primarily concerned with children who have not experienced good enough parenting in their early years, and as a consequence have issues around eating and food. We will explore the impact that poor parenting and trauma have on normal patterns of development, specifically in relation to food and feeding. If children have a disability that affects either their ability to process food or their ability to manage the eating task, this may require strategies specific to their particular disability and health needs.

Section II of this book includes comments on different approaches described by two families struggling with their children's eating issues.

SECTION I

UNDERSTANDING EATING AND FOOD ISSUES

JAY VAUGHAN AND ALAN BURNELL

CHAPTER 1

Normal development of eating and good nutrition for children

In this chapter, we discuss the various aspects of "normal" development of eating and good nutrition for children, which include:

- sensory motor development;
- the relational component of feeding; and
- nutrition.

As we will see, eating and good nutrition are important for a range of reasons apart from the nutrients they provide, which shows why this issue is so crucial for children.

When establishing what is "normal" development in this area, we need to be aware of different variations in food culture and food eating practices. This is significant if the child's eating patterns are at odds with those of the family they are living with (as is the case with many fostered and adopted children).

Sensory motor development

The sensory experience of eating begins in infancy with milk and all its nutrients.

Sensory integration is a term used to describe processes in the brain that allow us to take information we receive from our senses, to organise it, and to respond appropriately. From a sensory integration perspective, eating is a highly complex activity, which consists of numerous skills, processes and experiences (Le Révérend et al, 2014). Some of the key sensory processes involved in eating are:

- interoception;
- motor skills; and
- sensory experience.

Interoception

Interoception is an umbrella term, which refers to the process whereby the nervous system receives sensory information originating in the organs, tissues and cells of the body. This occurs at both a conscious and unconscious level (Khalsa et al, 2018; Bernston and Tsakiris, 2019; Martin et al, 2019), and includes the physical sensations of hunger, temperature, thirst, pain, breathlessness, heart rate, and emotional states.

Development of the interoceptive system starts at birth and is dependent on the attuned responses from the infant's caregiver (Tsakiris, 2017). For example, when an infant cries due to the interoceptive sensation of hunger, their caregiver uses their own interoceptive ability to attune to the infant's need and anticipate that they may need to be fed. If the infant is fed, and the feeling of hunger is dispelled, the infant comes to recognise the sensation of hunger; the repeated experience allows the infant to assign meaning to the sensation, enabling adaptive responses later in life. The ability to know when to eat and when to stop eating is influenced by receptors in the stomach, which are "programmed" by good enough parenting.

Motor skills

Once a child is able to detect the desire to eat when hungry, they must use the necessary motor skills in order to successfully carry out the actions of eating.

Milk is provided by the parent or caregiver, straight to the newborn infant's mouth. From birth, the infant begins to develop the oral motor skills required for eating, which involves co-ordination of sucking, swallowing and breathing to allow milk to be safely carried to the stomach. It is this co-ordination that ultimately leads the infant towards what is known as "readiness to oral feed" (Lau, 2015). This stage is easy to take for granted as instinctive, but it actually requires diligent and patient guidance by the parent or caregiver, which children coming into the care system may not have had.

Between the age of birth and six years, the child's mouth (including tongue, lips, and jaw) will undergo a number of transformations (Matsuo and Palmer, 2008). Research has identified that the sorts of foods infants are exposed to have long-lasting effects, with bone and muscle growth responding to the progressive exposure to harder textures (Le Révérend et al, 2014). Therefore, the food choices provided by parents and caregivers play a crucial role in ensuring muscle strength and bone development.

Appropriate weaning[1] experiences prepare the infant to develop the skills required for mastication (chewing), which involve a complex process of bone, muscle, teeth and soft tissue (such as tongue, lips and cheeks) co-ordination. Proficient chewing provides an array of nutritional benefits, ranging from nutrient uptake to influence on endocrinal pathways.[2] Therefore, the development of this skill plays a key role in a child's health and overall development that requires patient parental care and attention. (See also: NHS Weaning Guide, www.nhs.uk/baby/weaning.)

As children develop, they begin to gain the necessary skills to eat and drink independently. Postural control (the ability to maintain an upright posture) plays a critical role in this and begins with head control. Postural control is imperative for hand–eye co-ordination (Flatters *et al*, 2014), and therefore plays a crucial role in enabling children to use their hands to bring food to their mouths with their fingers, and later to control eating implements such as a knife, fork and spoon. Patient, kind and attuned caregiving is required for a baby to develop this.

Whilst postural control is fundamental to developing motor skills, children must also begin to integrate the sensory properties of eating (Ayres, 1972).

Sensory experience

Sensory integration is the organisation of sensory information from the body and the environment. Processing and co-ordinating information both internally and externally makes it possible for us to use our bodies effectively (Ayres, 1972).

---

[1] **The process of gradually introducing a baby to solid food while withdrawing the supply of its mother's milk or formula milk.**

[2] **A system of glands that work together and secrete different hormones to regulate the human body.**

Whilst the mouth serves as an effective food processor, it is also a complex sensing system, and one of the most nerve-dense areas of the body (Kutter et al, 2011). The process of chewing becomes a multi-sensory experience, involving touch, taste, smell, somatosensory[3] and auditory input (Prescott, 2015). Sensory perception is the individual's response to a sensation – whether they perceive it to be pleasurable or not – which is influenced by psychological, physiological and cultural factors, and which plays a crucial role in food preferences. This is significant for children who have had poor parenting or moved between cultures – they may respond to certain foods as not being pleasurable, linked to their earlier experiences.

During the weaning process, when a baby is gradually introduced to solid food, the child learns to apply the right amount of force when chewing, to co-ordinate the movement of their jaw, tongue and lips, and to move the food around their mouth in order to safely swallow. At a very basic level, taste and smell play a crucial role in helping humans and other animals to identify and eat food that is nutritious, safe and pleasurable, and they therefore also act as protective factors (Linscott and Lim, 2016). Whilst the taste and feel of the food in the mouth and the smell of the food belong to separate sensory systems, during the process of eating, smell and taste work in combination to create what is referred to as "flavour" (Spence, 2015). Hence, when suffering from a bad cold and being unable to smell, there may also be an absence of taste.

Food preferences begin in the womb, with flavours from the birth mother's diet crossing the placenta into the amniotic fluid.

---

[3] **Relating to a sensation (such as pressure, pain or warmth) that can occur anywhere in the body, in contrast to one localised at a sense organ (such as sight, balance, or taste).**

Infants are born with a preference for sweet and salty taste, thus sweet and salty foods have a greater likelihood of being accepted by infants when compared with bitter flavours, such as vegetables. Both infants and young children can learn to accept a greater variety of foods and flavours through repeated exposure.
(Birch et al, 2007)

It may seem hard to understand the relevance of all this information to children's eating issues, as most of us associate breast feeding, bottle feeding, weaning and the progression to solid foods as a normal developmental process. However, what sensory integration theory teaches us is that the ability to identify the feeling of hunger and to be able to operate the mouth muscles and tongue, and to process the sensory sensation of eating, requires the development of complex physiological processes. These processes are ultimately parent-led, which is the key point. If children have been neglected in infancy and subsequently placed in foster care or adopted, it is important to understand that these parent-led developmental processes may not have occurred or may have been in some way impaired. To use a simple analogy, children are not born knowing how to ride a bicycle; learning how to do it is a slow, parent-led task which probably involves progress from balancing on a scooter, to a bike with stabilisers and finally becoming an independent bike rider. The child then has to learn all the rules and protocols of safety when riding. This is not dissimilar from infants and children learning how to eat.

The relational component of feeding

Going back to the four pillars of parenting, eating and attachment come together during the first three years of a child's life. There are three key stages:

- In the first stage (birth–three months), the baby learns the critical sensory and sensory motor elements of eating.

- In the second stage (three–seven months), through daily parent/child interactions, which are not only based on feeding, the infant ideally develops a secure attachment relationship, to trust that their basic need for food and positive sensory-rich experiences will be met.

- In the third stage (six–thirty-six months), the child gradually gains the skills for independent feeding. This, as all parents know, is a messy business! However, over time, the child learns from the behaviour of the family and the culture of family mealtimes.

Culture may significantly influence the food experience for the child. It may determine not only the choice of infant feeding post-birth (breast or bottle), but also how and when the child is weaned (Hui, 2013). A key element, regardless of culture and types of food, is the emotional temperature that surrounds the feeding experience. If the emotional temperature in relation to eating is relaxed and nurturing, this will enhance the child's perception of food, eating and relationships.

From how you eat to what you eat – nutrition

Healthy eating and good nutrition are not only problematic for children who have had poor parenting in infancy and experience of the care system. A large national survey of 4–18-year-olds in Britain (Caroline Walker Trust, 2001), showed that the diets of a significant proportion of children and young people were:

- too low in iron, zinc and calcium;

- too low in vitamins A and C;
- too high in sugar and salt;
- not eating enough fruit or vegetables.

The nutritional aim for healthy eating is:

- five portions of fruit and vegetables a day (a healthy portion is usually regarded as equivalent to the size of the child's hand);
- starch-based foods are important for energy, so a healthy balanced diet should consist of one-third fruit and vegetables, one-third starch-based foods and one-third protein;
- a good variety of foods with adequate amounts of iron, calcium, zinc and vitamins A and C;
- low levels of processed sugar;
- packed lunches should have some starch-based food such as bread, but also meat, fish, cheese, egg, nuts or pulses, and two portions of fruit or vegetables;
- children should be encouraged to drink water or milk; unsweetened fresh fruit juice, which is rich in vitamin C, helps the absorption of iron. However, dentists mainly recommend water;
- that breakfast is a key meal and should not be skipped, and should contain protein and starchy food, but not sweet, sugary cereals.

The food requirements of children are age-related:

- **1–4-year-olds** require high energy food, but it is good to avoid high fibre as their stomachs are small and will quickly fill with fibre rather than more nutritional foods.

- **5–11-year-olds** require high levels of energy-generating food. Vitamin D and calcium are very important at this stage for growing bones and teeth, so full fat milk is recommended.

- **Teenagers aged 12–18 years** need high levels of calorific food to support growth and energy; they particularly need protein, calcium and vitamin D, iron and zinc; young girls during puberty will need higher levels of iron due to menstruation (Przybylka, 2016).

General tips on good food management

These are taken from the Caroline Walker Trust (2001).

- Increase activity before mealtimes to increase appetite.
- Sit at the table together as often as possible for family meals.
- Encourage children not to snack between meals. However, it can help to offer "little and often" meals for children who cannot manage long gaps in between. This is not the same as snacking.
- Follow a routine for mealtimes.
- If your child tends to fill up on fluids, offer them water in the middle or at the end of the meal only.
- Don't go overboard praising your child if they eat new foods or appropriate quantities, as this just highlights how important food is to you – instead, use gentle encouragement.

- Collaborate with your child over menus and shopping.
- Make mealtimes fun times.
- It can take 10–15 careful introductions to new food before a child will eat it.
- It is OK if an unfamiliar food just sits on the child's plate, as this will give the child a chance to touch and smell new food.
- Children are more likely to eat if they see others doing the same, particularly other children.
- Try offering picky eaters a special "taster plate" next to their regular plate – don't put expectations on the child, just let them explore it for themselves.

A more detailed account of the nutritional needs of children, by age and gender, as well as menus, is available in the Caroline Walker Trust report (2001), at www.cwt.org.uk and in a report by Przybylka (2016), found at: www.foodincare.org.uk which has children in foster care in mind. (See also NHS guidelines: Eat Well NHS.)

We are writing during the time of the Covid-19 pandemic, and evidence is emerging that uncertainty and disrupted routines are having a detrimental effect on children's eating patterns. It is not surprising then, that the majority of children who have come into the care system, as well as infants who have been subjected to losses and transitions, have some degree of difficulty with food and eating. Children may arrive in their prospective permanent families with the clear message that they have eaten well in foster care, and yet when they move to their new family, to everyone's surprise, they find it hard to eat what is offered. Other children, who were reportedly problematic eaters in foster care, settle quickly into their adoptive family's meal routines. It is hard to untangle this, but perhaps what is clear is that moving a child from one family to another is inevitably going to bring to the fore issues that children are only able to easily express through sleep, food and toileting problems, and of course, challenging behaviour. Often the distress of moving to a new home is initially enacted through food and eating. It makes perfect sense that a child on arrival in a new family should suddenly have extremely unsettled eating patterns. And one must not confuse adaptation with developmental progression. Many children who are, or have been, in care adapt, but at the cost of a more natural developmental progression.

CHAPTER **2**

The impact of trauma on eating and nutrition

A good deal of research has explored the impact of childhood abuse, neglect and trauma on children's eating patterns and nutrition. Rachel Cox and colleagues carried out one particularly pertinent review in 2016, from which we have summarised the key issues highlighted by research:

- **Chewing, swallowing and orientating food in the mouth**
  If your child is having difficulties with chewing, dealing with solids or swallowing, this needs to be addressed by a sensory integration and food specialising occupational therapist, because these difficulties concern motor skills, which have to be re-learned, rather than "acting out" behaviours. It is possible that some motor skill problems are not trauma-related, but due to the construction of the mouth, jaw and throat, so may require a referral to a specialist, which is done through your GP. Some specialist

services and advice on swallowing are provided by Speech and Language therapists in the NHS and privately.

- **Food maintenance**
  This includes hoarding and stealing food as well as overeating, which are patterns of behaviour resulting from childhood experiences of unpredictable feeding and food availability. It is very common for children who have been neglected and abused to hoard or steal food.

- **Binge eating**
  Another response to unpredictable feeding is binge eating, when children will eat everything they can, as in the past they have not known when the next meal is going to be available. Also, with poor early parenting, this group of children will not have learnt how to read the interoceptive information that their stomach is full. There are suggestions later in this book about how to manage this kind of binge eating, but if nothing works, it is important to consider whether your child has a genetic component impacting on their eating behaviour, such as Prader Willi Syndrome.[4] We would therefore recommend talking to your GP to get a referral to a specialist paediatrician and your child having a genetic screening blood test.

- **Comfort eating**
  Some children who have been neglected or abused establish a pattern of using food to comfort and regulate themselves. Children being drawn to particular types of high sugar, high fat and/or high salt food to "self-soothe" is a frequent problem.

---

[4] A rare genetic condition that causes a wide range of symptoms, including constant hunger, restricted growth and learning difficulties.

- **Pica**
  This term describes the eating of non-food substances. Pica is commonly seen in young children with Autism Spectrum Disorder (ASD) and other types of developmental disabilities. It is sometimes also an issue for children who have experienced early trauma. We have worked with children who, as babies, have had to eat their own nappies or wallpaper because they were so hungry and driven to eat to survive. It is not unusual, in our clinical experience, for children to continue this survival behaviour once they are living in a secure, food-rich environment.

- **Rigid food choices**
  Due to their early experiences, some children may develop a limited repertoire of food tastes and preferences from which they are reluctant to deviate.

- **Comforting fat and sugar**
  Trauma causes an increase in insulin secretion, which leads to a physiological need for fat-rich and sugar-rich food to counteract the stress response. This is not the same as comfort eating to regulate and manage emotions; it is about a hormonal balance needing to be restored.

- **Obesity**
  This is a more complex picture, with evidence that some children who have been traumatised do show signs of obesity, but other research has shown that obesity occurs more frequently in early adulthood and later in life.

In the light of infant trauma, eating patterns and the psychological significance of food, it becomes apparent why children who have had adverse early experiences can struggle with food. It is important that parents, carers and professionals treat the underlying trauma, and not the ensuing difficulties in isolation. The difficulties are a manifestation of learned patterns of survival in children who have had to take responsibility for their own food maintenance and emotional regulation.

Added to the above key issues from research, here are some observations from our clinical practice on the impact of trauma on eating:

- **Some children and young people struggle to sit still at mealtimes long enough to be able to eat and digest.** We know that animals that are on alert for predators eat whilst scanning their environment to keep themselves safe, and it is really much the same for these children. They are on alert, and literally not able to digest food as their system is prepared for action. There may also be a sensory or ADHD (Attention Deficit Hyperactivity Disorder) issue. If calming and regulating do not seem to work, then further sensory assessments may be required.

- **Other children and young people are still driven to explore their food and eat with their hands like a toddler.** Messy eating or not having learned the skills to manage the eating process of transporting food to the mouth and keeping the mouth clean can cause conflict and difficulties for the parent/carer and child.

- **Children and young people may become distressed if different foods on their plate touch each other, or by some colours of food, and will insist on how they want their food to be presented.** Again, this causes stress and conflict around food. The wish to control what is on their plate may be linked to early distress about being forced to eat regardless of their preferences, or regardless of whether food is appropriate or palatable. It is also a feature of children and young people who are on the autism spectrum, and may not be a specifically trauma-related behaviour but an indicator that further assessments are required.

The impact of trauma on nutrition and the child's capacity to absorb it

The Caroline Walker Trust (2001) strongly recommends that nutrition be regarded as a very important aspect of the quality of care that looked after children should be receiving, and that managers, social workers and foster carers (and, of course, adopters and special guardians) should all be trained on the importance of nutrition and how it should be delivered.

Nutrition poor to nutrition rich environments

Children in foster care, or who have been in foster care, will probably have made the transition from a nutrition poor environment in their birth family to a nutrition rich environment in their new foster or adoptive family. For most children, this is a smooth transition, although it may take time; but some children will have difficulties with absorbing good nutrition. Symptoms of this are poor physical growth, lethargy, and stools (poo) that are excessively smelly, sticky or light in colour. If, as a parent or carer, you have concerns about any of these issues, you should consult your GP, a dietician or nutritionist, as there may be some developmental issue or some residual infection in your child's gut or bowel.

Trauma and the need to keep blood sugar levels balanced

Research into adverse childhood experiences (ACEs, which include many events, like neglect and abuse, that looked after children may have experienced) (Larkin et al, 2014), found that ACEs have both a physical and mental health impact over a person's lifespan. These experiences cause high stress, and high stress levels affect production of cortisol (the body's stress hormone). For children who have experienced repeated high stress, cortisol production and cortisol levels tend to either burn out, and therefore not be available to the body, or they are constantly over-produced. Cortisol increases sugar in the bloodstream. Reducing sugar intake and sustaining high protein levels help to begin to restore balance in cortisol production. If children's cortisol production is out of balance, their behaviour will either be driven by adrenaline unmediated by cortisol, or excessively high cortisol production will cause lethargic behaviour. It is important when parenting a child who has had adverse childhood experiences and high stress in utero or in the early months, weeks and years of life, to think about keeping their blood sugar level as even as possible, with small and frequent meals, high in protein.

The body keeps the score

If, as a parent or carer, you are concerned that your child appears not to be developing physically, or that their physical development is unusual in some way, then do seek medical advice. We have learned from nutritionists that even when children are removed from adverse environments with poor nutrition, their bodies cannot always, for a variety of reasons, absorb the benefits of a nutrition-rich home – as Van der Kolk says in his book, *The Body Keeps the Score* (2014).

There is now considerable evidence that poor parenting and traumatic life experiences in infancy not only have a psychological impact, but also a physiological one on the child's bodily development and their ability to manage stress. Moving a child into a "good" home does not of itself completely address these issues, which can persist unless specifically addressed.

CHAPTER 3

A neuro-physiological understanding of eating and nutrition

Research has shown that looked after children have higher rates of problematic eating behaviours than their peers from similar socio-economic backgrounds, including children who have been maltreated outside the care system. In Australia, 77 per cent of foster carers reported that children in their care had eating problems (Savaglio *et al*, 2019). Children who have experienced emotional abuse, neglect, inconsistent care, or sudden and multiple separations were shown to have a range of eating and health difficulties, as well as a higher rate of insecure attachment behaviours, which are linked to eating and weight problems. Children can take to using food to self-soothe, and become self-reliant rather than relying on their primary carers to calm them. Neuro-physiology may be an unfamiliar concept to many readers, and may not seem immediately meaningful when thinking about food difficulties, but it can be very helpful in understanding and managing these issues.

What is neuro-physiology?

Neuro-physiology refers to the actual, physical structure of the brain, and what different parts of it do.

- The first and oldest part of the brain has been called the "**primitive brain**" or "**reptilian brain**". It oversees our body temperature, heart rate, digestion and breathing; it is therefore fundamental to thinking about food difficulties.

- The second structure is the "**limbic brain**", which amongst other things is responsible for processing feelings and memory. It is also the part of the brain that relates to others and helps us to develop relationships.

- The third structure is the **cortex** or "**thinking brain**"; its function is problem solving and being able to reflect and make sense of both the internal and external worlds.

To focus on eating, one needs to be **physiologically calm** (primitive brain), and in a **safe relationship** (limbic brain), in order to be able to deal with the complexity of nutrition. It is pointless telling a child to 'calm down' and to 'eat up', if their primitive brain is physiologically driving their behaviour, particularly if you have been exasperated and there is any hint of anger in your voice. It is not unusual for there to be parental tension at mealtimes when there are food difficulties. Parents and carers need to become the "thinking brain" for their child, and problem-solve what is triggering the child's primitive brain, because the child will probably not be able to know or articulate what is upsetting them. There are also issues that need to be considered in connection to the body and the actual task of eating – how the body works in order to actually chew, swallow and digest food.

A neuro-sequential approach

This simply means that you have to follow the neurological and developmental pattern or sequence, and calm the child's primitive brain, getting into a safe attachment relationship, and only then begin to think and talk about a problem.

All of us know that when we are profoundly distressed or overwhelmed, to sit down and eat a full meal would feel not just inappropriate, but it would be physiologically impossible to swallow and digest the food.

In the last 15 years, neuro-scientific research has taught us that when looking at child development, we need to take a holistic view that encompasses biological, neurological and psychological aspects in an integrated way.

Survival mode

If a child is still traumatised when placed in a new family, it means that they are at times operating in a "fight, flight or freeze" survival mode based in the primitive brain. A child may have been in foster care managing reasonably well, but the move to another family is highly likely to trigger their nervous system back into being unable to feel calm and safe.

When in such a hyper-aroused state, eating a meal may well be too difficult for some children, as their body would be physiologically wired to be on alert and ready for action, especially if "bad things" have happened at mealtimes in their past. For other children, feeling stressed may drive them to revert to craving certain sorts of food that helped them to calm in the past, or to eat constantly as a way of pushing all feelings away. Other children may literally not be able to swallow food or chew properly because they were not weaned by their parents and have not developed these skills.

If your child has not yet learned that their new world, their new family, and the adults in it are safe, then their body will continue to work in ways they used to survive their past traumatic experiences. This means that it is going to be really hard for them to be calm and settle to eat in accordance with the new family's culture. Every cell in their body will be sounding the alarm. We survive trauma by having such alarm systems in the brain and body. Shutting these systems down once they have been activated and put on alert is not easy.

We believe that an understanding of trauma is important in order to be able to relax and soothe a child – particularly a child who has been affected by trauma and loss in their early life. To begin with, we need to think about how to calm the child's body – the first step to parenting any traumatised child. Sadly, many adopted children have had stress hormones, drugs and alcohol processed through the placenta into their body even before they were born; they were not properly fed post-birth; weaning to solids was not appropriately done; and their nutrition was woefully unbalanced and inadequate.

CASE STUDY: SARAH

Sarah was four years old when placed with a single female adopter. In foster care, Sarah would only eat mashed food, and this continued into her adoptive family. She insisted on sticking her fingers into her porridge and smearing it all over her face as she sucked in great globules of it. Her adoptive mother added butter to the porridge in a desperate attempt to give her a balanced diet. She worried that Sarah was not eating enough, and that she was exhausted and grumpy once she started school. Family and friends all felt that Sarah was too messy an eater to sit with them at mealtimes and was a bad influence on their own children. They also offered lots of unhelpful advice.

Sarah's adoptive mother talked to her social worker, who referred her for specialist advice. She sobbed as she said what a failure she felt because she could not even manage to properly feed her daughter. Sarah's history with food was altogether sad. It seems that she had not even been bottle-fed, or very rarely, and then with a dirty bottle full of stagnant milk. She had pretty much moved on to McDonald's solids when only a few weeks old – not baby solids carefully mashed up, but bits of burger and chips.

That night, Sarah's adoptive mother went home and offered Sarah a bottle of milk to drink. Sarah was wary at first, but as the warm milk trickled down her throat she began to gurgle with joy. Over the coming weeks, Sarah moved from milk in a bottle to pureed apple lovingly cooked by her adoptive mother. Little by little, Sarah moved from baby food to finger food and carefully pureed solids. She was weaned as she had not been weaned before. It was hard because Sarah, it turned out, was understandably terrified of choking, and one can only wonder how many times she choked on McDonald's food at a very early age. She learned that this new mother made food that she could swallow, and then she gradually learned to chew. It took time and there were some backward steps, but Sarah learned to trust, and her mother learned that her big four-year-old girl needed to go back in order to go forward.

It should be noted that not all professionals adhere to the strategy of re-introducing bottle feeding. Our view is that reverting to a bottle may not be appropriate for every child, but can be therapeutic for a child who has had a traumatic history and needs to go backwards in order to go forwards. Children sometimes ask for a bottle, at some level aware that it is an experience they either missed or that was difficult for them. Bottle feeding, as well as having neuro-physiological benefits, can also have psychological benefits, particularly in relation to attachment formation. We would not recommend bottle feeding as a long-term strategy, but as an approach that can be linked to therapeutic life story work, helping the child to make sense of their early history.

Trauma, sadly, does not always end with a good permanent placement. The very process of coming into care and being looked after is traumatic. When children are removed from a potentially harmful environment, they have no way of understanding what may come next. They may move through emergency placements, short-term placements, respite care and sometimes failed placements. A history of multiple placements will leave a child trapped in fear and uncertainty about carers and their future. This sense of confusion and fragmentation is not helped when detailed information about the child's history is not shared with current carers, who are therefore unable to help the child make sense of their history. Even when that history is known, foster carers and adoptive parents may be fearful of referring to it as they don't wish to upset their child, and because they are often themselves distressed by the information. Any parent or carer in this position should be asking for professional guidance and assistance from a social worker or therapist as to how best to make sense of troubling information for themselves and their child. It is important to help your child to regard their eating issues in a developmental and historical context. It will help them not to feel ashamed or that the difficulties they are having are their fault.

In the *Australian Social Work* journal, the reviewers of an article, 'Therapeutic interventions for children with eating difficulties in the care system' (Savaglio *et al*, 2019) made the point that interventions needed to be trauma- and attachment-based, and to focus on 'the symbolic meaning of food and the processes around it'. The review aims to encourage carers to move away from thinking about food simply as a commodity or a tool of reinforcement or punishment, but as an important factor in helping children to recover.

Trauma and attachment-based perspectives need to be front and centre in the development and delivery of a problematic eating intervention for young people living in [alternate care] to treat their symptomatic behaviours and to address the underlying impact of their previous traumatic experiences.
(Savaglio *et al*, 2019)

The next chapter suggests how foster carers and adoptive parents can support their children in a holistic way, based on the most up-to-date research into the impact of trauma on child development (McCullough *et al*, 2016; Vaughan *et al*, 2016; McCullough and Mathura, 2019). This treatment model is called Neuro-Physiological Psychotherapy (NPP).

CHAPTER **4**

A step-by-step approach to eating and food difficulties

General principles for children who have been, or are, in care

As most food difficulties have their origins in infancy, carers and parents dealing with them should respond as one would to a young infant. But whilst parenting a baby requires attuned and soothing parenting strategies, parenting a traumatised baby is more complex because you need not only to be aware of, but also to understand, their primary experiences.

The focus for carers and parents with children who have food difficulties must be on **regulation** (primitive brain) and **attachment** (limbic brain). Life story work and making sense of the past, as well as problem-solving, require higher brain (cortical brain) thinking and are harder to access for children who are still stuck in "fight, flight or freeze" mode. So, in parenting a child with food difficulties, one has to be aware of the general principles of parenting a traumatised child, together with that child's specific history. It is this history that will inform the details of your strategies to help your child with eating issues.

Step-by-step guide to approaching eating difficulties and nutrition

Step 1: Developmental assessment

All children who have been in care should have a comprehensive developmental assessment. However, although all children in care have a health assessment that includes development, sadly not all of them will have had a comprehensive developmental assessment. New parents may have to insist on further investigation, as it is now recognised that there is a high incidence or possibility of the following conditions:

- developmental trauma
- Sensory Processing Disorder (SPD) or difficulties
- Foetal Alcohol Spectrum Disorder (FASD)
- Autism Spectrum Disorder (ASD)
- Attention Deficit Hyperactivity Disorder (ADHD)

The first two conditions (developmental trauma and Sensory Processing Disorder) are most common, in our clinical experience, but the other three also need to be considered. If you feel that your child has significant feeding difficulties and you have serious concerns about their weight as either under or over what it should be, then it is always important to talk to your GP or health visitor or to ask for a referral to a dietician or an occupational therapist who is trained in feeding approaches. An accurate diagnosis is a first step towards ensuring that appropriate support and funding are available, and appropriate strategies for home and school are in place to help your child to achieve their potential. If your concerns do not warrant medical specialist consideration, then continuing along the steps laid out in the rest of this chapter should provide you with a helpful framework to support your child and yourself. Food is of vital importance; a healthy diet with high levels of fruit and vegetables, and a low sugar, low salt and low fat intake is going to be important for your child's health in the longer term. However, babies and young children need full fat milk as this is important for myelination (the process that coats neural pathways in the brain with the substance vital for a healthy nervous system).

Step 2: Understand your child's food and eating history

The next step towards thinking about your child's food issues is to understand their history and to make some educated guesses about their experience of food and being fed, both in their birth family and in foster care (if you have adopted your child) or in previous foster care placements (if you are a foster carer). Food for a child who has been poorly parented and neglected can be a hugely complex and emotive subject. You may be able to find out about your child's food and eating history from their previous foster carers (if they have been in a placement prior to living with you), or from your social worker. There may also be some details in the adoption medical report, especially in relation to your child's birth weight. It would be helpful to consider:

- How was your child fed post-birth: bottle or breast?
- Did they learn to suck or did they struggle to feed?
- What was their birth weight, and did they meet the percentiles expected and put on weight post-birth?
- How was your child weaned?

- How available and appropriate was the food offered during their early life in the birth family?
- How nutritious was the food offered?
- What was the eating culture in your child's birth family and in previous placements? Did they eat at a table, or on their lap while watching TV? Did they have to scavenge for food or have to fight with siblings for enough food?
- How and what was your child fed while in foster care?

It may not be possible to gather all of this information, but sometimes your child's birth family history can give you a sense of what things might have been like, and you can make some "educated guesses" about the answers to some of these questions. Your child's current behaviour in relation to food and eating can also give you masses of rich information about what things might have been like for them before they joined your family.

CASE STUDY: RUTH

Ruth, aged eight, was creating havoc at every meal in her adoptive family; so much so that the family had got to the point of hating and dreading mealtimes. Ruth did everything she could to disrupt meals and, to the horror of her adoptive parents, she ate by stuffing food into her mouth with her hands. Ruth ate anything she could get hold of, and when out shopping one day even went so far as to pick dirty chewing gum off the pavement and pop it into her mouth.

It had become a huge battle, with her adoptive parents feeling that Ruth was ruining every mealtime. Amid the chaos of often spilled food or broken dishes, she would settle in and stuff food into her mouth as if she were starving. Ruth's adoptive parents sought help, and as part of this intervention more information was gathered about Ruth's history. The story that emerged was that Ruth, aged four, rang the police to ask them to read her a bedtime story, and when the police turned up at her birth family home, she was all alone trying to make herself a sugar sandwich with some stale bread. She was filthy and the flat was full of overflowing, rotting rubbish, and there was no food in the mouldy fridge. For the first time, Ruth's adoptive parents were able to make a connection between the chaos of Ruth's birth family and her current problems with food. A plan was agreed that involved engaging Ruth in planning and cooking the family meals, offering a snack plate that was always available to her, and her adoptive parents never leaving the house without food in their pockets or bag to prevent any further pavement scraping.

Step 3: Think about your child's current eating behaviour and relationship to food

A food diary may be a helpful way of getting a sense of your child's relationship to food and their eating routine over the course of a week.

- What are your child's food preferences and food dislikes?
- Are you worried that your child is not getting sufficient or the right nutrition?
- Can you analyse the quantity and quality of your child's food intake and nutritional balance?

- Does your child find it difficult to sit still long enough to eat?
- Is your child too stressed to digest food because their body is primed for action?
- Can your child not manage the process of chewing and swallowing, and therefore is it a sensory motor issue?
- Is your child anxious that there will not be enough food?
- Is your child stressed about food being bad or unpleasant?
- Is your child competing with siblings for available food?
- Is your child reluctant to try unfamiliar foods (more so than is usual for their developmental age and stage)?
- Do they try to control food because they feel, or have felt, so out of control about the rest of their life?
- Do you mediate your relationship with your child by using food to bribe or reward them?
- Does your child recognise that food is important to you, and therefore may be using food to either placate or antagonise you or other members of the family?
- Have mealtimes become a battleground that you dread?

If children are above the age of four or five, and able to have a relaxed conversation about their early life experiences, it can be helpful for you to explain the way in which these experiences may be a reason why they struggle with food, in order to give them some context for their feelings and to help them make sense of what is happening. It is best not to attempt this at mealtimes, but at other times of day when your child is calm. This will also help your child not to feel guilty, blamed or shamed for their difficulties and to begin to make sense of them. We cannot stress enough how important this step is – purely addressing your child's current behaviours, in our experience, ultimately does not work.

Step 4: Self-awareness and reflecting on one's own food issues as a parent

As well as thinking about your child's history regarding food and eating, it is important to reflect on your own and your family's history regarding food. What were your own childhood experiences with food and eating, and what challenges have you perhaps had to face? What was the culture in your family in relation to food and mealtimes, and what did you hope to emulate in your adoptive family – or hope to avoid? This process of reflection on your own relationship to food and eating is vital, as inevitably one's own history and issues are "triggered" when parenting, and if you are parenting a traumatised child, this is even more complex, as the trauma is literally imported into the new family.

Step 5: The need for regulation in relation to food and eating

Children who have been traumatised find that internal messages, their **interoceptive** messages, are not in sync with the external **extroceptive** information. So, when their stomach is rumbling, they may not recognise this feeling as hunger, and the smell of cooking may not trigger pleasure at the thought of food being prepared, but rather alert them that an emotionally charged eating event is approaching. Or they may not be able to tolerate their stomach rumbling, and need instant food if they are catapulted back to their early terror of no food being available. Mealtimes can become a huge trigger for all sorts of feelings stemming from your child's history. Their desperate wish for instant food or their revulsion around food is more than likely linked to early trauma. It is going to take time for the stomach rumble to be linked to the reassuring smell of lunch. However, it is possible for your child to become aware of their food triggers and internal cues, and to develop strategies for coping.

It is helpful to know that protein has a positive effect on reducing levels of aggression, and so can be used to help regulate your child. In our clinical practice, we give high protein food to children who are likely to become, or are becoming, dysregulated, as we know from experience that this will help them to calm. We would offer a combination of cheese, ham or houmous, with vegetable sticks or crackers, and fruit. As a parent or carer, it would be helpful to carry high protein snacks with you when out of the house with your child, or perhaps your child's school could be asked to give these snacks to your child at break times. We would not recommend giving just fruit by itself, which schools consider to be a healthy snack, as fruit eaten by itself turns to sugar (which is not good for your child).

There is also some research evidence that shows that Omega-3 fatty acids, which are found most commonly in oily fish like salmon, mackerel and sardines, can reduce levels of aggression in children and adults whose diets have previously been deficient in them (Gajos and Beaver, 2016). So whilst we are not necessarily recommending Omega-3 supplements, it would certainly be worth considering an increase of oily fish in your child's diet.

Parents and carers need to think "body" and think "nervous system". So, consider:

- your child's heart rate;
- your child's breathing;
- your child's skin temperature.

You may also want to track your own nervous system and note how your own heart rate, breathing and skin temperature are being activated. If you can regulate yourself, you will be more able to help your child to regulate. This is called co-regulation. The focus of the regulation needs to be first of all on your child's body.

Muscles need to be relaxed, or as much as possible, and the whole physical state of the body calmed. When the body is "pumped up", the digestive system is shut down.

Both over-eating and under-eating disorders have been found to be associated with difficulties in perceiving and interpreting interoceptive input (that is, the way the brain perceives things like hunger, thirst, or feeling hot or cold) (Martin et al, 2019). More recently, research has linked attachment style and interoceptive perception, establishing that those who have an avoidant attachment style have lower interoceptive functioning across a number of areas (Oldroyd et al, 2019). (See also Dan Hughes' book in this series, *Parenting a Child who has Emotional or Behavioural Difficulties*, for more information about attachment styles.)

The development of the child's interoceptive system is dependent on carers or parents enabling the child to assign meaning to their internal sensations – for example, learning to understand that their rumbling tummy means they are hungry. In the context of feeding, if a child is not fed in response to interoceptive cues of hunger (perhaps because they have been neglected or abused), then they may fail to develop accurate interpretations of bodily sensations and the ability to respond to them adaptively (Herbert and Pollatos, 2019; Martin et al, 2019; Oldroyd et al, 2019). In other words, for the child to know to eat when hungry and stop eating when their stomach is full can become problematic.

Behaviours associated with interoceptive difficulties
- Not knowing when they are full, leading to overeating.
- Not recognising the sensation of hunger, leading to a lack of nutrition.
- Interpreting hunger sensations as being painful.
- Becoming anxious around the sensations of feeling hungry or satiated.

Specific sensory integration strategies

- Encourage mindful eating, paying attention to the sensations experienced when eating.

- Talk as a family about how it feels when you start to feel full.

- Support your child to create a language around the sensations they feel when they eat or begin to feel full.

- Move away from depending on external cues to indicate fullness; do not insist that everything on your child's plate is eaten.

- Observe your child when you think they may be hungry: do they look tired, distracted, etc?

Step 6: Are the food and eating problems linked to motor skills?

Recent research has identified that the incidence of motor skill difficulties in children who have experienced complex trauma is five–seven times higher when compared to the rest of the population, and that exposure to sexual or physical abuse was most likely to affect motor skills (Wade *et al*, 2018). Such difficulties are likely to influence a child's ability to develop the motor skills required for feeding, including the use of cutlery, successfully bringing food to their mouth, or sitting at a table.

If children have experienced severe neglect or physical abuse and have been deprived of appropriate types of food, the development of their facial muscles will also be affected. Specifically, tongue weakness can result in food being trapped in the mouth; difficulties with chewing or moving the food to the back of the mouth in order to swallow can cause discomfort or gagging (Le Révérend *et al*, 2014).

Behaviours associated with possible motor skill difficulties

- Having difficulty in remaining seated at mealtimes.
- Using cutlery and food utensils – tearing at food rather than cutting it.
- Bringing food to the mouth – lots of food around the mouth or mess around the table.
- Difficulties in chewing food – taking a long time to eat, eating only part of a meal, or preferring soft foods.
- Swallowing – gagging on foods, or preferring smooth textures.
- Eating with the mouth open.
- Poor lip seal when using a straw or difficulty applying sufficient force to draw up liquid.

Specific sensory integration motor skills strategies

- Weighted cutlery can lead your child to have an increased awareness of their body.
- Modifying the task: if your child has difficulty cutting up food, present it in bite-sized pieces and encourage using a fork to spear it.
- Practise using cutlery at times other than mealtimes: while cutting up playdough or in imaginary play, like pretending to cook food and feed dolls.
- Practice oral motor activities such as blowing, sucking or biting – this helps to improve awareness of the mouth and improve oral motor control.
- A plate with a raised edge may help your child to load food onto a spoon or fork.

- Encourage your child to engage in gross and fine motor activities, and in exercise to improve posture and upper body strength.

- Ensure that seating at the dinner table is the right height for your child, with their feet able to touch the floor, their bottom reaching the back of the seat, and their elbows and knees at right angles. This may require a highchair with a footrest or a platform for the child's feet to rest on.

Step 7: Are the food and eating difficulties connected to sensory processing difficulties?

It has been found that sensory processing difficulties (the way we perceive touch, taste, smell, etc), which often occur in conjunction with other diagnoses such as ASD or FASD, can affect eating and mealtime success (Twatchman-Reilly *et al*, 2008). Other research has identified that children who have experienced significant neglect often have difficulties with sensory modulation (Wilbarger *et al*, 2010). Sensory modulation refers to the intensity of the sensory input that an individual experiences when eating. Difficulties in this area often result in sensory input being too intense (hyper-reactivity). This may mean that the taste, smell or touch of food is perceived at a sensory level as being unpleasant, resulting in avoidance of certain foods.

Two patterns have been identified in relation to sensory hyper-reactivity and the impact it may have on feeding (May-Benson and Goodrich, 2018):

1. ***A defensive pattern*** is characterised by experiencing significant discomfort during everyday encounters, which can include aversive responses (dislike) specific to mealtimes, such as the sounds of cooking, the smell of food, and the acoustics in the room where the child is eating.

2. ***An oral defensive pattern*** refers to individuals who experience sensory hyper-reactivity specifically in and around their mouth; they may show aversive responses (dislike) to different textures or tastes, resulting in:

   — refusal of certain foods;

   — anxieties about different foods on the plate touching each other or being "contaminated" by each other;

   — extreme responses to smells or tastes, e.g. gagging, vomiting, distress;

   — a preference for bland foods due to over-sensitivity to taste or smell;

   — a preference for very strong flavours due to under-sensitivity to taste or smell;

   — a preference for smooth or soft foods due to over-responsivity to texture;

   — a preference for crunchy or chewy foods due to under-responsivity to texture.

Specific sensory integration strategies

- Take note of the foods that your child enjoys: the texture, smells, taste and the sensory changes the food undergoes as it is chewed, and attempt to offer foods with similar qualities.

- Engage in oral motor games with your child, such as blowing bubbles or using straws to play "cotton wool football" prior to mealtimes, to prepare your child's mouth for the sensory experience of eating.

- Reduce the noise and visual stimulation within the room in which your child is eating.

- If your child is under-responsive, provide food with strong flavours and crunchy textures.

In relation to Sensory Processing Disorder and difficulties, it may be helpful to consider asking your GP to refer you for a specific sensory integration assessment.

Step 8: Attachment and food issues

When thinking about food and eating difficulties, you also need to think about the "emotional temperature" of family mealtimes. We humans are social beings, and we tend to eat in relationship to others. If your child's early feeding experiences as a baby and/or young child were scary or unpleasant, then this immediately sets up a problem for them. Babies who were force-fed or fed rancid milk can struggle to eat when older. Children who have been starved and have had to scavenge for food can be on constant alert and never confident about where their next meal will come from. Young children only have so many ways of communicating their distress, and food is a good way of expressing feelings, often leading to carers or parents being caught up in a desperate battle to get them to eat.

Family meals should be regular and frequent and should create a healthy attitude to food. Therefore, if mealtimes have become a source of stress, it is vital to find ways to calm the emotional atmosphere in relation to food and eating.

In the first place, be aware of what is happening. It may be that for a while, family meals will not be helpful for your child or family. You may need to "go backward to go forward" and feed your child one-to-one, until they are able to cope with feeding themselves in a family setting. You may even want to consider a much sloppier diet, like weaning, especially if weaning was not a good phase for your child in their past. It is important to see this as a positive step rather than an irritation, as one-to-one spoon feeding and a playful approach to food is part of the attachment-forming process between carer/parent and child.

Try the idea of a taster plate with your child. Allow them to sample food without pressure to try anything if they do not wish to.

The food culture of a child's prospective permanent family may be very different from the food preferences of a child, and it can be hard to marry them together in the early stages of a placement. You may have to move towards allowing your child to eat the food they are familiar with, and only gradually introduce other items. This could take several months, and it may be that your child is never going to feel comfortable eating everything you would like them to eat. The aim is to move towards a balanced nutritional diet that takes into account their experience of food and any physiological impediments.

It is important to be aware of the complexity of your child's attachment relationships. How can you help them to know that you are a safe and to-be-trusted adult? It is also important to bear in mind that children in more established placements, who feel that they can trust their new parent (their "secure base"), may, at times of heightened stress, lose this sense of safety. It may therefore be that your child is less able to access you as their "secure base" at mealtimes, when stress responses are more likely to be triggered based on their early memories of mealtimes or eating.

Many fostered and adopted children have what are considered to be "disorganised" attachments, meaning that their attachment strategies are not necessarily consistent, and when stressed, their disorganised strategies will come to the fore. They may oscillate between fearful, controlling, angry and avoidant behaviour, making it hard to understand them, and even harder to support them.

One of the positive results of establishing a healthy relationship to food, eating and mealtimes is that it becomes part of the basis of forming good attachments, which generalise into day-to-day social interactions. Eating is not just about good nutrition, but about social interaction and relationships.

Step 9: Reflect with your child on food and eating issues

Talk to your child about food issues at other times than during mealtimes; help them develop a reflective and curious approach to their problems around food and eating. This could involve helping them to see the links between their early history and their current difficulties. It is important not to push your child to talk if they resist or feel overwhelmed by this sort of discussion. It would only be helpful if your child is willing to tease out with you why things are the way they are, and what might help to make them better.

In many ways, this is like life story work, and all part of helping you and your child together to think about their history and origins. It requires both you and your child to be in a calm, regulated state, and relating to each other, so that higher brain reflective thinking is possible without the child being triggered into a trauma state. It is what has been described as "being curious" together (Hughes, 2013).

This higher stage of brain function is not just an attribute of older children; it is a capacity that children of all ages have when they are in an optimal, quiet but alert state. Parents and carers, perhaps with some assistance, need to find the right age- and stage-appropriate words to discuss distressing life events and why they may be hindering your child's good relationship to food. It is important to be mindful that if a child can reflect on their food issues when they are calm, it does not mean that they can access this higher brain thinking when they become stressed at mealtimes. Dealing with food issues is a slow and gradual process, and understanding "why" does not necessarily or immediately solve the problem. However, it provides a framework, which can generate a meaningful dialogue between carer/parent and child.

Step 10: Adolescence and food

The issues around food and having a healthy well-balanced diet become considerably more challenging if your child is an adolescent. At this age, it is no longer possible or appropriate for you to control their food intake as you did when they were younger, and they probably have much more freedom and money of their own to make food choices.

There are a number of potential flash points, including getting them to have breakfast in the morning before school/college or at weekends/holidays when they want to sleep in until lunchtime. Lunches on a school day can be a combination of being too busy to eat at all, making poor food choices from the school canteen or buying inappropriate chips and chocolate instead. All in all, the child whose diet was well managed can become a very different person in relation to food at the moment they move to secondary school. Along with adolescence come issues about identity, body awareness, acne and all the agonies of wanting to look a particular way and fit in with a particular group. At the same time, adolescents need high levels of calorific food to support their growth and a number of important vitamins and calcium as they grow.

All of these issues are more marked for a child who has been in the care system. As a carer or parent helping with these preoccupations, it is vital not to get into a huge food battle with your adolescent.

So, what can you do, faced with a resistant young person?

- Avoid battles you will not win; fighting about food with your adolescent risks creating more problems around food that can become entrenched and lead to an eating disorder.

- Know that eating disorders can be an issue for boys as well as girls.

- If breakfast is an issue because your young person just wants to dash out without eating, consider giving them a healthy muesli bar or offering a protein-filled milkshake.

- You cannot control what they eat when they are out of your home, but you can make sure that you have a quick-fix, healthy, but desirable snack for them the moment they arrive home, which will avoid the hunger-driven row that could otherwise ensue.

- Whilst you might wish to cook your usual family meals, consider factoring in meals that you know that your adolescent likes and will devour.

- If you want or need to cook something that you know your adolescent will not like and is unlikely to eat, make sure that you have a back-up offer of a quick sandwich with their favourite filling as an option, and never offer this angrily.

- Consider the possibility that your hungry adolescent might need supper with the family, followed by a late night second supper or substantial snack, as they may have to make up for a lack of food during the day or just simply be growing and need more.

- Consider a general multi-vitamin supplement to make sure that your adolescent gets all of the necessary vitamins and minerals.

- Try to give your adolescent full fat milk, as calcium is so important for their growing bones.

- Encourage your adolescent to cook for the family and offer to be their sous chef.

Food difficulties

- Encourage your adolescent to be active in meal planning for the week; this needs to be an enjoyable activity and highly praised.

- Have emergency food available for them that is high in protein and vitamins, and is an easy hunger fix.

- Get medical advice from your GP if your adolescent develops worrying food issues or food phobia, or shows dramatic weight loss or gain.

CHAPTER 5

Frequently asked questions

In this chapter, we look at some of the frequently asked questions that carers and parents may have about particular food issues affecting their child.

Should I change my child's eating habits when they are first placed with me?

Every child placed in a new family after a series of moves is going to be confused and stressed. As adults, we know that when we are stressed, we often revert back to old ways of managing, and this can include our eating patterns. If a child has learned in their previous families that eating is an all-day grazing process, or that food is always eaten in front of the TV, then it is going to be hard for them to shift, and it is going to take time. So, it may be that at first some meals are shared in front of the TV, and later at a table near the TV, and then as things ease, the TV can be switched off.

At times of stress, it may be that your child will be desperate to revert to the comfort of eating in front of the TV, and this needs to be considered not as a backward step but as a pause. It could be a good opportunity to acknowledge to your child that you know they are stressed and that things have been hard, so it is just fine to watch TV and eat together today.

Should you keep to the diet your child had in their previous placement, even if it ends up with family members having different meals at different times? It is good advice when children move to a new placement to minimise the trauma of change and separation by keeping to the routine they know. However, the diet your child was used to may, in your view, not be nutritious, or appropriate for their stage of development or for the rest of your family. First of all, work out what would be a suitable range of foods and menus; then, in an age-appropriate way, begin to talk with your child about improving their diet and enhancing their well-being step by step. Clearly, carers/parents need to remain in charge and make the decisions, but some degree of negotiation works best. Giving your child choices – either of which you would find acceptable – is one strategy. So, for example, instead of asking 'What would you like for breakfast?', ask 'Would you like eggs or porridge for breakfast?' The aim has to be to enhance your child's diet and to enable them to engage in enjoyable food sharing and mealtimes. The process needs to be a gradual adaptation, based on your understanding of your child's early experiences and their current struggles with food, towards the desired goal.

What if my child cannot eat meat or food that requires a lot of chewing, and only wants sloppy, mushy food?

As we know, some children may not have developed the sensory motor skills to chew, swallow and digest solid food because of poor parenting in infancy. As a new parent or carer, you may have to go back to an earlier developmental stage with them. This may even require feeding your child for a time, rather than allowing them to self-feed, which can disrupt family mealtimes but will encourage attachment. This is effectively a re-weaning process; you may have to begin with purely soft food, gradually include finger food, and ultimately move to more lumpy food that requires chewing. If this process does not appear to work, it may be that your child has oral sensory motor difficulties (as described earlier in this guide), which require further investigation.

Should I let my child help themselves to food?

Much will depend on your own family "rules" and how they are understood and observed. Who can help themselves to what, when, with or without asking first: snacks from the fridge, fruit from the bowl, sweets from the jar? When is helping yourself not the same as stealing? Be aware of your own attitudes toward food and eating, and mindful that this is unfamiliar territory for your child.

Children who have experienced both emotional deprivation and food deprivation (as these two are often inextricably linked) require a clear structure so that they know when the next meal is coming; having food that is always available for them to snack on is vital too. It is of course important that the snacks are food that you want your child to eat, and so a sweetie jar or biscuit tin are not desirable, but a fruit bowl or special cupboard with healthy snacks is a good idea. Children who have been starved in the past can find it very hard to wait for meals, so in the early months, and even years, of placement, being able to eat little and often can help. Because children who have been traumatised are driven to desire sugar, salt and high fat foods, snacks ideally need to consist of combinations of fruit and protein, as this will prevent an uneven blood sugar surge and support their adrenal system.

It is understandable that children who have experienced starvation will be driven to take food from the fridge or kitchen cupboard. Probably all children have at times sneaked an extra biscuit, but for the traumatised child who has experienced life-threatening hunger, the urge to take and hoard food is high. It is better not to be disapproving or to have constant food discussions, but when calm, to engage your child in reflective thinking about their issues with food and how this may link to their early life experiences. It is important that your child has some understanding of the historical context of their eating problems.

Why is my child becoming more rather than less "picky"?

When our child first came to live with us, she would eat everything and say it was delicious, but now she is very picky.

In foster care or in their birth family, some children develop compliance as a survival strategy. It may seem paradoxical, but when your child starts to become "picky" about food, it probably means that they are learning to trust you not to hurt or harm them, and are able to "protest" or express a preference. So don't be alarmed by this sudden expression of an opinion about food. Perhaps by offering two, or a maximum of three choices, you can enable your child to exercise control while maintaining the nutritional integrity of their meal.

What about the infant who does not want to give up the bottle?

If children have been traumatised in infancy, it is more helpful to think about developmental stages than chronological ages.

In our experience, it is not uncommon for a child, even in middle childhood, as they learn to trust their new parents or permanent carers, to regress to wanting a bottle, possibly at bedtime, if it is offered in a nurturing and affectionate way. If your child has arrived in your home still being bottle fed, then it may be hard to let it go as a source of security. Obviously, you want to ensure that your child has a balanced diet, but perhaps there is no rush for them to give up this comfort, and they can make a gradual transition to the weaning stage.

It is also important to consider dental health and speech development when weighing up these issues. You do not want your child to be sucking juices or sugary drinks, as they might have done in infancy, because it would damage their teeth. Having significant dental treatment as a young child can be traumatic. So it is all about balance and supporting your child to get their needs met without having a teat continuously in their mouth. Bottle feeding should be reserved for a special cuddling time with a parent.

How should we deal with adolescent eating fads?

Adolescents need high levels of calorific food to support their growth; they also need a number of important vitamins and calcium as they grow. It can be hard to maintain your adolescent's balanced diet, as once in secondary school, they are increasingly out of your control and orbit. This means that a healthy nutritious breakfast and evening meal become even more important. Being an adolescent is stressful, and adolescence may bring up many issues from the past for children with a traumatic history. Bear in mind that having to manage secondary school as well as changing hormones is likely to mean a reversion to some toddler challenges, including demands for comfort food. So what appears like an adolescent fad might actually be a stress response and an attempt, through food, to regulate their anxiety. Food can easily become a battleground, and avoiding battles with your adolescent is really important, as you are unlikely to win and more likely to alienate your young person.

Why is my child permanently hungry and why do they eat until they are ill?

Children who have been poorly parented have often not learned how to interpret information from their stomachs. Good carers or parents regularly feed their infants, knowing that they must be hungry, and pick up their cues when they are full. This helps a child to recognise their bodily sensations. You may have to assure your child that 'Your tummy is probably telling you that you have had enough' before they have had too much.

It may also be that your child is eating too quickly for their brain to receive the message that they are full, as it can take up to 20 minutes for this message to get from the stomach to the brain. It can help children to have crunchy food before a meal, such as carrot sticks or celery, possibly with a dip, to slow down the eating process. It will always help if children know when the next snack or meal is coming, that there will always be more food so that they don't have to eat everything in sight, and if they have been literally starved in the past, that there is enough food in the home.

Why does my child hoard food – sometimes in the strangest places?

If children have been starved in their early lives, it makes perfect sense to them to hoard food in case there is none later. It can help a child who is hoarding to have a box of healthy snacks that is just for them and that has their name on it. They may wish to keep

this snack box in their room or elsewhere, and this might need
negotiating as you may not want them to eat in bed. A child who
hoards food may also respond well to having a meal planner for
the week so they know what food to expect on each day. Talking
about the link between hoarding and past experiences will help
your child to understand their own behaviour.

CASE STUDY: JANELLE

Janelle, who was adopted as a baby, had experienced food
deprivation in her first few weeks and had failed to thrive.
When Janelle became an adult, and more so when she
became a parent herself, she was obsessed with having
sufficient food in the house. This reached the point where
she needed to have two full-sized fridge freezers in her
kitchen constantly fully stocked. Janelle's family would
gently tease her about it. But even though Janelle knew
the origins of her hoarding behaviour, she chose not to
stop it; as an adult, she found her own way of managing
her anxiety about not having enough food.

Why does my child never seem to be hungry, and hardly eats but snacks all day?

Some children who have experienced trauma are so wired to
being on alert that it is really hard for them to settle and eat. If the
body is getting ready for "fight, flight or freeze", then the digestive
system is not ready to eat a full meal. These children find it easier
to snack and have a "little but often" approach to food. The first
aim must be to reduce their stress response to enable them to eat
a meal. Exercise before mealtimes to calm the body and encourage
the appetite would be important for such children.

It is also important to initially go along with small, regular meals to ensure that your child is getting enough food and to give them the message that there is no food shortage. Think about what your child eats, so that they are not "snacking" but eating a series of balanced mini-meals.

Why does my child crave sugar and anything sweet?

Children who have been traumatised can easily develop a craving for anything sweet as a way of helping their body to feel calm and comforted. Sugar can emulate the calming effect of the hormone cortisol, so it makes perfect sense that stressed bodies crave sugar. Unfortunately, we know that the effect of sugar does not last long, and can lead to a crash when the sugar burst ends. Sugar is hidden in many foods we buy, and even fruit containing natural sugars can be an issue. The good news is that combining fruit with protein means that the fruit sugar does not behave like sugar, and is better for the body.

If your child is a sugar addict, very gradually replacing sugar with healthier alternatives is best. To maintain a good blood sugar level, we recommend moving to regular and frequent small meals with balanced sugar, so that the craving is gradually reduced. It is interesting to note that it is thought that babies like sweet food because it acts as pain relief for them, which makes one wonder if this is why traumatised children can get stuck with craving sugar.

Why does my child constantly crave hot, spicy food?

Interestingly, whilst children can crave sugar to calm their bodies, they can also crave hot, spicy or very salty food as a way of regulating their system. As with any food craving, it is hard to stop, and the aim should be to achieve a gradual transition to a balanced diet. It would be important to note when your child craves this kind of food, as it can reveal what causes stress, and in time this would be something to discuss with your child.

It is important here to be aware of your child's cultural heritage and the variety of foods they may have been used to in previous families and placements. If your child has a different cultural background from you and your family, then we would suggest that you don't only try to accustom them to your tastes and food preferences, but that you also embrace some of their cultural food preferences. In so doing, you will acknowledge cultural differences in a positive way.

Why can't my child sit still long enough to eat?

If your child finds it almost impossible to stay still to eat, you need to think about their over-activated nervous or sensory motor system. It may be helpful if your child can exercise before a meal, or you may find other ways to help them to become calm enough to eat. If calming your child before a meal fails to reduce their over-activity, it could be an indication that it is a sensory motor regulation problem and requires a sensory integration assessment. ADHD may have to be considered, although unfortunately, a lot of ADHD medication has a side effect of reducing a child's appetite.

Why will my child only eat certain foods, avoid specific colours and consistencies, and control how food is presented on the plate?

It is not unusual for children who have been traumatised to be controlling about a range of things, including the food they will eat and how it is served on their plate. This could be because their experience of food has been limited and it may take some time before they feel safe enough to expand their food repertoire. One way to resolve this is to have taster plates so that they can experiment without pressure.

It may be that a child's dislike of a certain food consistency is linked to their early poor weaning experiences, and they may need to go backwards and be re-weaned before they can manage some food textures.

Whilst it is not uncommon for children on the autism spectrum to struggle with food colour and keeping different foods separate on the plate, it is also not unusual for traumatised children with difficult early food experiences to have issues about the colour and look of food. The challenge for carers and parents is to work out how much is trauma-related and how much is a sensory or developmental problem. As a rule of thumb, it is always worth beginning with the developmental issues. If it is not a straightforward developmental issue, the next thing to consider is a link between current behaviour and past experiences of eating, before moving on to sensory processing and oral motor issues, with the help of a sensory integration assessment.

How can we rule out/assess/get help for conditions like anorexia, diabetes or obesity?

Finally, if all aspects of developmental stages, sensory integration and trauma re-enactment have been explored, but your child's behaviour persists, then the more complex diagnostic possibilities need to be explored. It is a common myth that a symptom of undiagnosed diabetes in children is sugar craving, whereas actually the symptoms are thirst, weight loss, abdominal pain and vomiting.

However, children who are obese and eating lots of sugar are of course at risk of Type 2 diabetes as adolescents and later in life.

If your child is seriously over-weight, or not eating, or general health/growth is causing serious concern, then always seek medical advice. Sadly, many young girls, and boys too, develop eating disorders and these are hard to treat, but early intervention is key. So always trust your instincts if you are worried, and seek specialist advice.

Conclusion

Here are some do's and don'ts that sum up the advice provided in earlier chapters.

Overall do's and don'ts

Don't

- Don't treat the eating problem without treating the trauma.
- Don't be afraid to go back in order to go forward.
- Don't turn food into a fight, but into fun.
- Don't bribe or coerce your child to eat.
- Don't shame your child for overeating or hoarding.

- Don't set up rigid rules around food and eating that are not sustainable.
- Don't talk about food and eating issues all the time.

Do

- Do have a clear timetable for meals, a meal plan and snacks for the day/week.
- Do collaborate with your child over menus.
- Do engage your child in shopping and cooking.
- Do ensure that food is available little and often.
- Do encourage water intake.
- Do increase activity before mealtimes to stimulate appetite.
- Do sit at the table for family meals as often as possible.
- Do reduce expectations if there is a problem, and work towards a gradual improvement.
- Do provide taster plates and allow food to remain uneaten on the plate.
- Do be kind to yourself, as managing the complexity of food and eating issues is hard!

A final thought

It is our belief that helping children who are fostered or adopted to eat well is also about helping them to recover from significant harm, neglect, abuse, multiple losses and transitions, and enabling them to form meaningful and loving attachments. We hope that parents and carers will see that helping their children to

Conclusion

have a healthy attitude to food, and a healthy diet, is intimately connected to helping their children to fulfil their potential to grow and develop.

Food is vital for our capacity to cope with everyday life and to manage life's stressors. The importance of food should never be underestimated. If you eat well, you live well! If it feels hurtful and rejecting when your child refuses to eat the food you have lovingly prepared, or "plays up" at mealtimes, try and remember that what is really happening is that they are making you feel like they have felt at other times in their life. Food and feeding are emotive and challenging for parents and carers, so be kind to yourself and know that it is hard to help a child who is struggling with food issues. However, we know that with time and care, and attention from parents and carers, it is possible for children to develop healthy eating patterns and to thrive.

SECTION II

PARENTING CHILDREN AFFECTED BY EATING AND FOOD ISSUES

A window on Harry's world

Jo Jackson

The early years and formative experiences

I had been approved to adopt twice, by two different agencies, for one or two children. I wondered whether I was ever going to be "allowed" to be a parent, and then they brought me "Harry" (not his real name). His Child Permanence Report, or CPR – the document that describes the early life of a child waiting to be adopted and their trajectory through care – was light on detail, but it was clear that there had been Children's Services involvement since before he was born and that his young parents had struggled to manage, with the phrase 'poor home conditions' featuring several times, along with there being 'little evidence of food in the property'.

Harry raced through a series of foster placements after he was removed from home by the police aged two, and there were references to him becoming 'extremely stressed' around mealtimes, at home and at nursery. In one foster placement, he would 'sometimes search for food after he had eaten' or have 'extreme tantrums if he was prevented from having unnecessary snacks' and 'when he was told "no"'. During contact, both parents apparently struggled to offer consistent boundaries and there was a reference to them using food as a means of regulating their children's behaviour. Here, again, Harry would become 'highly stressed'.

Harry and his sibling had been removed from significant risks in their birth family, including drugs, weapons and domestic abuse. In his final foster placement, separated from his sibling, it appeared that his tantrums and extreme behaviour had been resolved; the only reference to food being the statement under 'Health', that Harry was 'not a fussy eater'.

I'd done a lot of reading and spent time with friends' adopted kids, so I felt prepared. Food was my thing, and because of other details in the CPR, it was at that time the least of my worries. It seemed obvious to me that Harry was going to need to know that there would always be food at our house. This wasn't going to be a problem. Friends have always joked that my house is the place to be during a crisis – and Covid-19 lockdown has proved this beyond doubt. And Harry, I believed, at four, was old enough to communicate when he was hungry and to accept reassurance from me. The other thing that came up in discussions with his last foster carer was that withholding[5] was an issue. I read up

---

[5] Term used for when children try to avoid going to the toilet, often due to constipation and a build-up of stools being too hard or painful to pass.

on it in a really useful book by Anthony Cohn called *Constipation, Withholding and your Child*, and used it to plan my meals for "introductions week" at my house. I was determined to resolve this problem through diet, without resorting to medication. I thought that would avoid Harry feeling a loss of control, and it becoming the battleground that the foster carer confided it had been.

The two weeks of introductions were exhausting but wonderful. I had already fallen in love with Harry before I met him, and he didn't disappoint. He was engaging and full of personality – and remains so. The first time I took him out on my own, he sat in the back of the car taking every item out of my bag – which I'd packed for every eventuality – and seemed to relax, as if he'd established that I was competent to look after him.

In the week before he moved in, I brought Harry to my house every day. As well as making a two-hour round trip to pick him up and then again to drop him off, I structured the day around food, which came at set times and included items to reach a specific fibre count. Harry sat on the loo regularly every day and did his business; I thought I'd got a plan that worked. All we had to do was carry on.

So that is what we did. Luckily, Harry genuinely wasn't a fussy eater, in the sense that he'd eat a wide range of foods. I guessed that this was one result of being effectively starved as a young child. With firm and consistent boundaries, food became a shared joy. Since there were just the two of us, we always sat down to eat together. Food structured our day, and became a key tool for attachment. Harry's palate was amazing; he could identify individual ingredients and often started or ended his meal with comments like, 'This is delicious'. I remember at some point saying to professionals, 'Thank God he loves food, because if he made it a battleground it would make my life a misery'. Harry ate plain yoghurt, muesli, any kind of fruit, many vegetables, curry and almost anything I cooked. He seemed to understand that my food was an expression of love.

For years, mealtimes were sacrosanct. Harry sat at the table chatting with me – eating with a knife and fork. The only rule was that if he didn't finish his main course, he couldn't have dessert. I stuck to this rule, and as a result he rarely failed to finish, even when he tried to say he didn't like something. On the rare occasions he really couldn't eat something, I didn't put it on his plate again. What I marvel at most, from this distance, is that we had dessert with every meal! Those days are long gone.

What became clear over time was that Harry struggled to distinguish bodily sensations such as hunger and thirst from emotional reactions such as sadness. I'd read about this, and worked hard to help him identify key differences and name bodily sensations. This kind of therapeutic approach was a major part of our relationship from the very beginning, and was made possible by the fact that there were only the two of us, with no one competing for either of our attention.

I realised that I needed to instil strong, healthy habits for the future. Coke and other fizzy drinks were out, along with fast food like McDonald's and KFC. We would eat out at independent cafes and restaurants reasonably frequently, with a view to coaching Harry about how to manage social situations involving food, which he'd struggled with in foster care where, I discovered, frequent buffets had him refusing to limit himself to one choice of dessert. Limiting choices seemed to help him manage, and though he'd "try it on", I rarely experienced what I considered real problems with behaviour around food. I always followed through when I said 'no' or set a limit.

The structure I imposed did limit us in some ways: it meant that we needed to come away from social situations early because Harry simply couldn't handle becoming hungry or in any way "unmoored". And he couldn't really handle long periods without close supervision from me or another adult. He had very low self-esteem and seemed to "unravel" without me.

School: the importance of communication between adults

As Harry got older, he would ask before taking a drink or food from the fridge, though he was allowed fruit on demand. There were always mid-morning and mid-afternoon snacks, and warm milk at bedtime to help with sleep. We had food licked, it seemed, which was just as well, because there were quite a lot of issues at school, and by Year 2, I was in daily communication with staff, and had half-termly meetings with the SENCO (Special Educational Needs Co-ordinator).

At age seven, after a long fight, I managed to get Harry seen by clinically qualified professionals. Cognitive tests ruled out ADHD and depressive illness. Harry was diagnosed with disorganised attachment disorder.

At school, Harry usually had a packed lunch, which allowed me to manage his diet to avoid constipation. In the early years I signed up for school milk, and the school would give everyone a snack, usually fruit. When Harry was discovered pilfering the excess fruit left outside the classroom, it was met with amusement. I was alert, however, because issues of control and manipulation were evident in other areas by then. Any gap in communication between the adults around him, or if he felt he'd got away with something, could quickly lead to risky behaviour, because it made him feel unsafe and he would try to exert control.

At the end of one term, in Year 2 or 3, I got a letter reminding me to pay for Harry's school dinners. There had been a few periods when I'd signed him up for school dinners, but this hadn't been one of them. It turned out that Harry had just joined the queue and told the canteen staff that I'd forgotten to give him lunch. Fortunately, he'd only done this the week before the holidays. I paid up, but the school agreed that in future Harry would only get school dinners if I asked for them in advance.

Similarly, at the before-school and after-school club Harry attended to give him more play time, but also to give me a bit of a break, he would sometimes eat four rounds of toast in the morning after he'd already had breakfast at home. Clearly, left to his own devices Harry would just eat and eat.

By Year 4, when Harry was nine, he was really struggling at school; he would spend all his break and lunchtime with a member of staff. At a school meeting, it became clear that he was cadging food off every adult he came in contact with, and they were giving him some of their lunch. While we could laugh at his resourcefulness and charm, and speculate that members of staff gave him food because they liked him, and it was something positive they felt they could do for him in the face of other intractable problems, it was necessary to shut this down.

Soon I was getting a phone call from school staff around 1.30pm every day to say that Harry couldn't manage at school, and I would go to pick him up. What didn't emerge then, was that lunchtime for Year 4s and Year 5s was later, so that Harry now had to wait until around 1.30pm to eat. He was starving, and he couldn't cope. Who knows if this made any difference to what happened next? Probably not.

In the Year 5 spring term, the local authority decided that Harry needed to go to a special school. My preference was for him to stay at the same school until the end of Year 6 to avoid what he would experience as another rejection, and to give me time to find an appropriate secondary school. It was not to be. In May, it became clear that Harry simply couldn't cope, and it was no longer safe for him to continue at the school. We did our best to create a positive ending for him, but the school agreed when I made the decision to keep Harry at home while I looked for a school he could start in Year 6.

No school: the impact of uncertainty, and regression

I said earlier that "Harry" is not his real name. He asked me to call him Harry, after Harry Potter, with whom he identifies strongly. Like Harry Potter, Harry believes that he is cursed, pursued by evil and unable to escape a fate determined by his birth. This means that he experiences intense fear, due to early trauma, which he struggles to regulate. Even in familiar places, such as school once was, he is waiting for a terror-figure to appear. That is the main reason he couldn't cope at school, and the main reason he struggles now.

The appropriate school was never found. It doesn't exist. Harry's challenging, sometimes violent behaviour means that he would be placed in a school run on a "sanctions and rewards" system. According to CAMHS (Child and Adolescent Mental Health Services), that would have made his difficulties 'more severe and more acute'. Harry has not attended school since, but I didn't know then that this would be the case. And I fell into the same trap that Harry's school fell into, and relaxed the rules about food.

There were two reasons for this. The first was that I wanted to compensate for Harry's sadness and distress; and the other reason, later, was that I was busy looking for a school and fighting for help from the local authority. There was the occasional Coke or KFC, not all the time, but enough. And there were more things, like ready meals and sugary treats. But it was only temporary, while I was overwhelmed with paperwork and research into schools. Until it wasn't.

Mothers, in particular, will tell you about parental guilt, but adoptive parents have a special relationship with it. I can still wonder whether I just haven't tried hard enough, have tried too hard, made the wrong decisions, caused Harry's problems, or made them worse. But the connections between Harry's behaviour now and the behaviour described in the CPR are obvious, and probably my intense focus early on meant that they were so well managed that it seemed they had actually been "fixed". They hadn't.

Harry has always struggled with autumn, the start of the new school year, but more importantly, the time he was separated from his sibling while in foster care. In 2017, I was preparing for a tribunal regarding Harry's EHCP (Education, Health and Care Plan), when miraculously, Harry began to play outside with a group of mainly boys who lived locally and whose parents I knew a little. I had feared that Harry would never be able to do this, so it was a bit of magic I wanted to support. I bought Harry a watch – digital, as he'd never been able to learn to tell the time using an analogue clock – and we set an alarm for him to come home to eat.

A lot of the time this worked well, and I could make sure that he was fed and watered. I often had to adapt my timings to match those of his friends' families, because if he didn't come back for lunch, things would often go wrong. Fallings out and even physical fights could start, and Harry could become very reactive and take off on a bike, which wasn't safe. Harry knew that he would find it more difficult to manage his reactions and his behaviour if he didn't eat and drink at the right time, but obviously, it was hard for him to leave when he was absorbed in having fun. I took to driving around the local area looking for him with a packed lunch, so that he would be fed even if he wouldn't come in. However, there seemed to be more to it on occasion, almost as if he was sabotaging himself to ensure that he couldn't manage. It was as if something inside him compelled him to make things difficult for himself, so that he couldn't just have a good time.

Harry's friends thought that he was lucky not having to

go to school, but of course Harry didn't. His self-esteem was at rock bottom, and he would seek conflict. He wanted to stay out as late as his friends, and sometimes wouldn't come in at teatime. It became very difficult to maintain any kind of structure without that provided by school. It was like one long summer holiday, with no anchors, no mooring.

Harry was also experiencing different food cultures at his friends' houses, and would want what they had which, if he was to be believed, consisted mainly of "beige food" from the freezer, takeaways and fizzy drinks. He became increasingly belligerent about food and now simply helped himself.

Around the time that Harry left school, we received an assessment report from a specialist organisation that had been commissioned by the local authority after several years of forceful advocacy by me. Part of this was a sensory integration assessment, which, among many other issues, identified that Harry was under-responsive to tactile stimulus, and that this affected not just his eating sensations, but Harry's whole digestive system and evacuation, thus giving insight into his withholding as well as his difficulties with interpreting physical sensations related to hunger and thirst.

We had begun work with this agency at Easter 2018, when Harry was 11 years old, with fortnightly, full-day sessions. Whenever we arrived, the team would bring Harry a snack box with his name on it. This was designed to allow him to self-soothe, but also to create the perception that this place and these people were safe and could anticipate and meet his needs. They had to hide the rest of the food in the kitchen, as Harry would otherwise raid cupboards throughout the day. This was unusual. Apparently, the snack box was enough for most of the adopted or fostered children with whom they worked.

In 2019, Harry had a major quarrel with his closest friend and he simply stopped playing outside. There were increasing outbursts at home and Harry began to display really extreme behaviour around food. His table manners were increasingly regressive; he took to eating with his hands – if he would come to the table at all.

Up until then, Harry had often taken food, but typically would leave some for me. Now he would just take and eat the whole meal, as though he didn't care whether I had anything to eat or not. The most worrying thing, though, was the binge eating that started at this time, with Harry putting on about a stone in weight in as little as three weeks. He also became very emotionally volatile, and would search for food during or immediately after an outburst. He came to me one day with livid purple marks under his arms and across his belly, terrified that he had some terrible disease. I was shocked and worried. A Google search suggested that they were stretch marks, which I'd never heard of in children. It felt like a form of self-harm.

Increasingly, it was necessary to hide food from Harry if I wanted to keep something for myself or if I wanted to have a particular ingredient available for baking. Harry could tip the house upside down to find food, and when he did, he would eat the lot. I often only knew what he'd eaten by the wrappers I'd find dropped behind the sofa or his bed in a half-hearted attempt to hide them.

What was particularly hard for me was that food is a big deal for me. I like to grow it, make it, experiment with it. Now if I baked biscuits, Harry would simply eat the lot in one go, usually late at night. If I tried to stop him, he would become violent. He was like a six-foot-tall two-year-old having a tantrum. I repeatedly threatened to stop buying chocolate, ice cream, desserts, or baking, but who wants to live like that? And anyway, by now I was much less consistent at following through, and he knew it.

CAMHS threw us a lifeline at about this time, and I took it. They had made a "pragmatic assessment" of ADHD for Harry, and were suggesting starting him on methylphenidate, a drug that would allow him some control. Harry wanted to take it, and the effects, even on a low dose, were immediate. On the first day, Harry said, 'If I'd had this, I could have managed at school'. Perhaps he could have.

A side-effect of the medication was that it suppressed Harry's appetite; the binge eating stopped, and Harry gradually lost weight. Mealtimes became a lacklustre affair, with Harry pushing a half-full plate away and saying he was full. All the joy seemed to have gone out of food for him, and for me too as a consequence. Although the medication effectively controlled some of the most difficult aspects of Harry's ADHD and trauma-related behaviour, the loss of our family food culture was a high price to pay.

Worse, on days when Harry didn't take his medication – and particularly if I didn't know whether he'd taken it or not, as he sometimes lied about it – the schedule that I was trying to put into place was upturned. Harry would be continuously hungry and massively volatile.

In an attempt to mitigate this in some way, Harry and I discussed and then agreed with CAMHS a trial of a shorter-acting medication, so that the effect would wear off in time to eat together. Things improved a little.

And then came the Covid-19 lockdown, and gradually everything collapsed.

Lockdown: the world is not a safe place after all

At first, there was the fear of the coronavirus, confirmation of Harry's trauma-belief that the world is not a safe place and that adults can't keep you safe; then, the fear that this situation will never end and he'll never get back to normal. Harry has gradually stopped leaving the house. He hasn't been out for a month, and now has no desire to do anything other than play with friends on the Xbox – one of the few positives from this period – and eat.

Unsurprisingly, this has been a period when it has become increasingly difficult for Harry to manage his feelings. The physical activity that is absolutely necessary to his regulation has totally gone. His sleep pattern is all over the place: he sometimes wakes at about 8.30am; at other times, I'm shaking him awake for a Zoom session with his therapist at 11am.

And of course, I am struggling myself. While Harry is engaged with friends on the Xbox, and refusing or unable to participate in family mealtimes, lockdown has been a very lonely affair for me. At times, my ability to withstand what he throws at me, and my capacity to think creatively about how to help him, have been compromised, and the energy levels required to provide nutritious food at just the right moments to help him regulate have been hard to find.

A typical day might start with me waking Harry and trying to persuade him to eat breakfast and take his medication while he's verbally abusing me. But on other mornings, he's asking me to rub his back and tells me he's never going to let go of me. I never know which Harry I'm going to find. Often his first request (or demand) is to have time on the Xbox (which is governed through an app). Once on the Xbox, he typically won't eat or drink if he's taken his medication, especially if I am trying to get him to come to the kitchen table.

I tried leaving him to it, because he was perfectly capable of getting something to eat if he became hungry later. The problem with this was that he wouldn't come off the Xbox until teatime after not eating or drinking for seven or eight hours, and would immediately erupt into a dysregulated state that would quickly escalate. He would become threatening, and rampage around the house. I was so busy dealing with this bizarre behaviour and trying to help him regulate that it took me some time to realise that his behaviour was related to being hungry. Harry certainly wasn't aware of it and might continue to refuse food until much later, or he might provocatively seek food by repeatedly coming into the room and saying, 'I'm going to get some food,' in a tone of voice that made it clear he wanted a fight.

I've learned that the best thing is not to engage. This is hard, because every time he helps himself to food, he'll leave the kitchen in a mess, as well as picking the most unhealthy food, and vast quantities of it – a whole tin of biscuits, a tub of ice cream. If something is intended to be a meal for two, he'll eat it all.

Preparing to write this piece on Harry has really helped me focus. I looked back at the CPR with its descriptions of behaviour around food. Although the details are light, the parallels are clear to see. Food had been used to regulate Harry's behaviour, perhaps with bribes, perhaps with food being withheld. There was a high level of anxiety around mealtimes; Harry would become extremely stressed and sometimes search for food after he had eaten or have extreme tantrums if he was prevented from having unnecessary snacks.

Harry's first two years were in a house that was chaotic, full of violence, with terrifying and unpredictable people around, 'little evidence of food', and competition for attention and resources with his siblings. He would have lived in a constant state of fear, arousal and vigilance. He's 13 now, six foot tall, full of raging teenage hormones he can't control, and he's in the middle of a pandemic that appears once again to put him under threat and without agency to do anything about it.

So I determined to make sure that he wasn't hungry when he came off the Xbox. This was not as easy as it sounds. The food had to be portable, able to be eaten without leaving the Xbox, while lying down and using his hands, but without the dog eating it if he left the plate sitting on his chest, which would have caused an outburst. And it needed to work without any co-operation at all from Harry!

On days when he hadn't taken his ADHD medication, this would have to happen repeatedly, as Harry was then like a baby gannet, opening his mouth only to issue instructions to bring him food. And there were the days when he would pretend that he'd taken his medication. When Harry lied, it was like he was doing it "intentionally" (he was compelled to), in order to set up a fight later. There were clues if I paid close attention: how he was speaking to his friends on the Xbox, his volume levels.

This has been relatively successful, but there are still days when nothing works. Harry will come to the table and create a situation so that he can storm off, back to the screen. You'd think it would be obvious, but it always takes a while to see the pattern. And sometimes he'll start a fight just so that he can go on a binge. He's a traumatised child, stuck in patterns laid down in his brain and body as a baby, or even in the womb. Whether he'll ever be able to regulate his own relationship with food successfully is an open question, but I'll keep trying.

Reflections on the future

I am lucky to have some great professional support. An expert team I can talk things through with to check my thinking and my strategies, to focus on avoiding Harry feeling as if he's starving. And to give myself a break – it's OK to serve up a ready meal sometimes, even if he eats mine as well – fewer calories for me. And CAMHS, with whom my most recent discussion was whether we are entering bulimia territory and, if we are, what the key things are to do and not to do: avoid making him feel shame about food (a hard ask) and keep an eye out for signs of purging, just in case, though probably this won't be Harry's style. And celebrate little wins, which may actually not be so little: the 14-vegetable miso soup he loves, discovering Brazil nuts in his muesli, getting prebiotics down him, and some of the conversations we can have when he's in a reflective mood.

It's hard to balance Harry's genuine need for a high calorie intake, as a teenager who's already six foot tall and still growing, with the attachment issues that are evident in his relationship with food, sensory issues and a desire for a taste of adolescent independence that he genuinely can't handle. But it's worth it for the moments of connection, like when he comes in bombastic and rude, but I know that he really wants a cuddle, and I make him laugh by saying so.

Our latest venture is a mini-fridge. It's a take on the snack box idea. The obvious problem with a snack box is food hygiene, and I really wanted to get away from a bed full of discarded wrappers, crumbs and dribbles of various soups and so on. The basic idea is that the food in the mini-fridge is totally under Harry's control: I put it in; he decides what he eats and when. The hope is that he'll then leave the food in the main fridge alone, and this will help him to limit his intake. He won't engage in discussions about what goes in, as he wants what I choose, to prove to himself that I understand his likes and that I love him. Sometimes he simply eats everything in his mini-fridge and then raids the main fridge and kitchen cupboards as before, almost as if it had triggered him rather than regulated him. We have talked through the need he has to sabotage every good thing as soon as he gets it. We haven't found out yet how to make this work, but we said that we'd just carry on and try again, which we have. One thing sticks with me about the discussions we have had. Harry said, in a moment of insight, that what he liked about his mini-fridge was that he would know that whatever was in there, I wasn't going to eat any of it; it was all for him. Perhaps this is a reflection of having to compete for scarce resources as a toddler when there was little food in the house. This makes it worth trying to make the mini-fridge work. It might just take some time.

What would make a difference? Who knows? A bigger family? Certainly, that might make Harry feel he was missing out if he didn't come to the table for meals, but if there were other people around, would it feel like just another fight to get enough?

I'm going to make an analogy with raising and training a dog. I hope you won't be offended at the comparison. Traumatised children are so stuck in their primitive, instinctive brain that I think the comparison is fair, and in this family, we value dogs. A puppy is totally focused on its owner, and a Labrador, like our dog, is biddable, very trainable, and responds to all positive attention. But when the dog hits adolescence, you wonder what's happened and if you ever trained the dog at all. Then, as the dog matures, you see that your training was effective after all, and you have a lovely well-behaved dog who is happy. I'm holding onto this for Harry. I'm really hoping that the early work will reveal itself later to have been effective, to have enabled him to feel secure and happy.

Harry knows about growing food (I have a (neglected) allotment), food production, healthy food, food science, food labelling, food politics generally. He knows where food comes from and what healthy food looks like. For now, I have to hope that I've done enough. I hope that in time he will be able to make decisions around food that make him feel good about himself.

I know that it's not my fault Harry has food issues. I'm not being punished for thinking I'd got food – or attachment – licked. And if food becomes a battleground between us, it's not personal, even if it feels like it. And it's not your fault either, whatever your child's issues are. It's hard work to keep to a plan when your child sabotages it or can't manage it. It's hard work to make another plan when the first plan, or the second, or third, doesn't work. But keep going. Find a really good and empathetic professional to help.

I love Harry. He's in a family and, because of him, so am I. That's enough. We're doing the best we can.

Authors' comment

What shines out from this account of Harry and food is how loving, devoted and tenacious his adoptive mother has been. In our clinical experience, this is not untypical, but sadly this tenacity is often required of adoptive parents because basic assessments have not been carried out on their child, and consequently support has not been put in place. The simple message here is that without assessments, the appropriate support cannot be provided.

It is clear that Harry could and should have been diagnosed with sensory processing difficulties and ADHD, as well as developmental trauma, prior to his adoptive placement. This would have provided a structure and pathway for therapeutic intervention and would have assisted his adoptive mother in her attempts to address his eating difficulties, as well as his other challenges. What is striking is that a great deal was known about Harry's early traumatic birth family and fostering experiences, but no one helped his adoptive mother to make sense of it in relation to his eating difficulties. Luckily, she was able to use her own intelligence and creativity to make sense of his behaviour, herself.

What this case also illustrates is that Harry's adoptive mother managed to stabilise him during his early years with her, but with the stress of school and the onset of adolescence, Harry reverted to some of his earlier difficult patterns of behaviour. It was only then that she, and he, began to get the type of therapeutic help that they needed. In our view, this could have, and should have, been available much earlier on and would have lowered the risks that inevitably occur during adolescence for such a traumatised young person. This case study is a tribute to the extraordinary resilience and courage of a loving adoptive parent.

A pocketful of mashed potatoes

Daniel Swanson

Background

Prospective adopters have to decide which challenges they feel capable of taking on regarding possible adopted children. There is always a reason why a child needs to be adopted, and that usually involves trauma and emotional scarring.

My husband William and I feel very lucky to have found an agency near to us in North London, which specialises in post-adoptive care, but also prepares prospective adopters before they adopt, rather than only fixing what is broken. We spent the better part of a year plumbing our souls, as well as learning about a variety of likely traumas and difficulties that may come with adopted children.

Some conditions, we decided in all honesty, we wouldn't be able to handle. Others, like neglect and trauma, seemed like something we could manage, thanks to our training and personal backgrounds. Taking on a child with a challenging background and giving them a happier, more stable life was part of the appeal for us. We knew those scars would never disappear, but on the other hand, believed (and still do) that with the right support from us and experts, a child we adopted could have experienced trauma in their first few years and still flourish.

When we found George's profile on the Adoption UK website, we were hooked. Due to a history of domestic violence, and issues surrounding security, we didn't even see a photograph for the longest time, but we felt that his personality would match ours, and his background was something we could take on. When we first saw his profile online, George was three-and-a-half, and due to circumstances beyond our control, he was aged four when we finally brought him home.

Little George came from a more or less single-parent household. His mother was young when she gave birth to him. She and his birth father were in an on-off relationship: leaving George frequently on his own when they were "on" and exposing him to a high level of domestic violence when they went "off" each other. It seems from the reports and stories that there was a culture of heavy drinking, cannabis use and violent brawling. Sometimes that meant George was left on his own overnight in a highchair in the communal garden. Once the police found him, totally alone, in a dirty nappy, digging though the garbage looking for food. At another time, he was on his own in a room, eating all of the leftover pizza from the adults' party the night before, surrounded by the rest of the party's detritus.

Sometimes there was food in George's early life; it seems from all accounts that usually this food took the form of adult portions of very high-calorie, high-fat, salty takeaways. Sometimes there was no food at all. In that case, any living body does the same thing: it eats when it can, as much as it can, because who knows when the next meal is coming. Hot, spicy vegetables, meat, anything, it didn't matter, he wasn't picky – food was food.

The social work team's plan

Strangely, this way of eating a lot, or nothing at all, led to George appearing to be overweight. Perhaps technically he was – doctors thought so, social workers thought so, and the foster family agreed.

It's hard not to let your own issues around food come into play when looking at a child. How many times are we judgemental of parents or carers when we see a child drinking a soda, or eating fast food? Looking at George, doctors and social workers decided that he needed to lose weight, and they needed a game plan.

There were many concerning issues in George's background, but it seemed it was the "food thing" that gave his social care team the most immediate concern. There were multiple incidents in George's early life when the police had been called, or when he'd been covered in his mother's blood in public after parental fisticuffs. We've had discussions about probable consumption of alcohol in utero and overall neglect.

George's birth family was so volatile that social workers didn't feel safe going to the home themselves and sent the police instead. These were all other issues that would need to be addressed in time. Leading to, and during the introduction period, it was the food/weight issue that was the main immediate concern for the social workers, doctors and foster carers. I suppose George's weight was one thing that could be "fixed" in the short term – thus the diet. The first thing most adults do when they're trying to lose weight is to exercise more, and restrict their food intake or go on a diet. That may work for a time, but doesn't address the psychological or physiological root of the problem.

But it really was a concern! Whilst not obese, George was on the pudgy side. However, it was less the physical issue for the social workers and foster family, but more about his incessant hunger and obsession with food. George would tell anyone who would listen that he was hungry…even as he stuffed his face with whatever food was within reach. Even months after we brought him into our lives as our child, George would pick food up from the floor, street and from in between cushions on the couch or in the car, and if it wasn't completely decomposed, George would eat it, or try to eat it.

There was no stopping him; apparently food was all he would talk about. Even before our first heartbreakingly beautiful introduction, we were warned: 'He's going to tell you he's hungry – don't believe him, he's fine, he's eaten already', and 'He's had breakfast, snack and lunch so far today, don't give in'.

The problem was – George was hungry! With the best of intentions in the world, social workers, doctors and foster carers had put a three-year-old on a somewhat restrictive diet after living a life of feast or famine. George would have limited quantities of rice cakes for snacks, fruit and veggies, water, soya milk. All good things, but a finite amount of them, and rarely any "treats" or second helpings. Don't get me wrong, George certainly wasn't starving any more; he had three meals a day and snacks in between, but it didn't address the larger problem. The real tipping point for us was when we saw George at a birthday party during our introduction period; it was a no-holds barred feeding frenzy, like something off the Discovery Channel! Handfuls of cocktail sausages, chicken drumsticks, hamburgers, hot dogs, crisps, cake and cupcakes – as much as he wanted, because it was a "special occasion". Again, this little boy was being offered feast and famine, and food was a reward.

Taking a chance: our long-term strategy

Unless there's a fundamental and permanent shift in what you eat and why, "going on a diet" is at best a short-term solution. Adults do or do not stick to their own diets based on willpower – a child is utterly dependent on adults for the food that is given to them. Technically, yes, the diet was working, George was losing weight, and within the system, it really wasn't the time or place for the foster family or social services to take that deep dive into the source of the problem, but we knew that we would have to. Not to mention the fact that listening to a child constantly state that he's hungry is exhausting! Another thing we noticed was that George ate at different times from the rest of the foster family. Of course, most modern families don't fancy sitting down for dinner at 5pm, especially those with older children, but for George it reinforced the idea of food and loneliness, or food equating affection. Despite being safe now, with meals provided at a set time, he still wasn't experiencing a positive model of how people eat. Hilariously, George used to be able to tell the time in relation to when meals and snacks were served...but that's something he didn't hold onto, and we're having to re-teach: we may have missed a trick there!

George had a constant fear about food, and where food was coming from. Tragically, he once returned to the foster home to find it aflame, fire brigade in attendance and all. Most children would worry about the fire, or their toys, or even be interested in the fire fighters; not George – he merely asked, 'Can I have a sandwich?'

Even before introductions, we turned to our adoption agency for help. We knew that all the other issues – neglect, abandonment, etc – were equally, if not far more, important in the long run, but food needed to be addressed first. Our agency recommended the book *Love Me, Feed Me*, by Katja Rowell. Much like *The Great Behaviour Breakdown*, written by Bryan Post, which was our other manual, *Love Me, Feed Me* stated that we had to fix the root of the problem if we ever wanted to move past this food issue and get to what were, in our minds, the more pressing matters. We had to re-wire George's brain, and the best way to do that was to overcome the fear that there wasn't enough food, and to show him how people eat when they're not afraid.

On a deeper level, for George being fed meant being loved. When his birth mother was around, she was eating, and George was being fed. When she wasn't around, or wasn't being attentive to his needs, he would starve. It really was "love me, feed me" in George's brain. In foster care, there was consistency and affection, but not a culture of plenty.

When it came time to create our introduction book, we were encouraged by what we had learned to include photographs of a full refrigerator, as well as a table laid with a feast. We also included photographs of our friends' children holding food, and mentioned that their father or mother was an exceptional cook. When we made our introduction video, we did the same: showed a full fridge, lots of food; showed that there's always enough.

We wound up loving George's foster family, and they're a part of our lives to this day. Although seemingly quite different from us, we share common ground in caring about this little boy. But they, and his social workers, were decidedly not in favour of our radical plan, which was: give George as much food as he wants, as often as he wants it. The theory was that eventually he would realise there would always be food and he had nothing to be afraid of. We looked at their diet plan as tyrannical, and they viewed us as inexperienced hippies.

We had to play by everyone else's rules during the introduction period, which was extremely difficult! We held back on our desire to impose our ideas on this experienced foster home, but then gave George plenty of healthy food when we were on outings while getting to know one another.

It was all very exhausting. There were so many layers to a boy so young – but we were sure that food was one issue we could actually fix with enough dedication, compassion, and, as it turned out, stubborn-headed faith in the training and advice we'd received.

As every adoptive parent will be able to relate to, bringing George home for the first time was the most vertigo-inducing experience of our lives! On the one hand, we were overjoyed – finally, the moment we'd planned for (in theory) for over a year; and on the other hand, suddenly all of the theoretical issues were real, and we were responsible for the life of a gorgeous, traumatised little boy. We ran ourselves ragged, trying to make a good impression; to prove that we were fun, loving, entertaining and permanent. It was also the time we'd been waiting for in relation to the food issue: re-wiring the part of George's brain that said he wasn't safe, there wouldn't be enough, and all of this goodness and stability would end.

White-knuckling it – from theory to practice

I so vividly remember the first step: we produced the most enormous dish we had, laden with pasta (with tons of vegetables mixed in, so we could tell ourselves that if he was going to stuff himself, at least part of it was healthy!). And stuff himself he did! His eyes grew wide as saucers when we laid the dish down in the middle of the dinner table and asked if he wanted some. It was as though George had died and gone to heaven when we re-filled his plate as often as he asked. As he shovelled food into his mouth, literally hand-over-fist, he asked for more, even as his plate still had enough food on it to sate most children of his age. We simply said, 'Of course'. To say that inside we were "white-knuckling" it would be an understatement: were we doing the right thing? Sure, we'd read about this, and discussed it at length between ourselves and with our support team, but in practice it was terrifying! Were we simply paving the way to a different unhealthy relationship with food? Would he ever stop eating once he started?

We kept saying phrases like, 'There's always food in this house', and 'We always have enough to eat', and 'You'll never have to be hungry again'. We would make sure to always eat together as a family, and say things like, 'That was delicious, I'm full now' about our own meals when we had had enough.

At the time of writing this, George has been with us over four years, more than half his lifetime, so memory fails on what exactly happened that first evening. I do know that we kept filling his plate, and I do know he neither exploded nor ate the entire platter of food... though he did his best! I remember that at one point he asked for yet another plateful, which we gave him, and when the plate was once again full, he said the words we'd been hoping to hear: 'Can I save this for later?' As has happened many times since, and still happens on occasion, filling his plate or bowl when his stomach is already full, but something in his life is making him feel uneasy, is a way for George of making sure that there is more food, and he's still safe. In that case, George almost always eats a bite or two, then says he's full. Now, four years on, this "fill the plate to be sure" behaviour happens far less frequently. When it does, however, we know that there's something on his mind that's bothering him or making him uneasy. It's a handy signal for us, as parents, to give George special attention or to say, 'I wonder how you're feeling about...? I would think you might be feeling...?'

'Can I save this for later?'

On day one, we had done it...well, we hadn't cracked it, but we'd taken the first step, and it felt like a major triumph, and partial validation!

'Of course', we said, 'It will be there whenever you want it.'

William and I looked at each other and both let out a breath we didn't realise we'd been holding. It was not going to happen overnight, but it was the start on the road to recovery and repair for this little boy. With our help and consistency, he was already learning to regulate himself.

Boundaries, rules and self-regulation

Although giving George as much food as he wanted, whenever he wanted it, was our motto overall, we did develop ground rules. We would attempt to eat at home as much as possible. Having been neglected for so much of his early life, and then not necessarily eating meals with other people, his table manners were more akin to survival strategies than tool-using. We understood that having been left on his own so often, George sought and needed tactile experiences: sand pits, gravel, dumping Lego all over the floor, eating mashed potatoes with his fingers, etc. It looked like making a mess, but they were all (also) sensory-seeking behaviours.

Considering George's difficulties with food, the messiness and always wanting more, restaurants were more trouble than they were worth, and certainly weren't relaxing! We could control what went into the food we were offering at home, and we would avoid traditional processed sugar in baking (which I did a lot of to encourage our mutual attachment). Coconut sugar, agave nectar and honey became our only sweeteners. We learned to avoid having overly sugary foods in the house at all, which wasn't really an issue for us. It's one thing to find that a child has eaten all the cheese Babybels, another to realise that they've eaten a whole packet of chocolate biscuits! It was only when I made a disastrous birthday cake a year after our introduction (it looked like a spinosaurus dinosaur swimming and slowly dissolving in a vat of nuclear waste) that I finally caved in and used icing sugar for the first time.

Looking back, I think that we made the right decision regarding processed sugar. If it was obvious to us when George had eaten something that turned into a form of sugar as it was digested (i.e. bread, apples, etc), then it was triply obvious when he ate something with processed sugar in it. As we'd learned in our training and from reading, sugar in the blood stream produces a similar chemical to the one our brain produces when we're afraid. That's why a sugar rush looks so similar to panic. As adults, we can rationalise that feeling, but for a child with regulation difficulties, naming and dealing with different emotions was a stretch too far for some time.

Self-regulation was an issue across the board for George. It wasn't just food: George had a massive temper, which he only began to show us after the "honeymoon period" of his early days in our family wore off. Screaming, shouting, hitting, punching, kicking, head butting, biting – all of those things were possible, especially when we tried to assert boundaries, and more especially if those boundaries related to food. We knew that this came from a lack of regulation by his birth parents in his early years; he was merely acting as an infant or young toddler would...although at four years old, he was already a sturdy little boy, far larger than other kids his age at nursery. Some of his actions were clearly connected to the aggressive behaviours he had regularly witnessed when he was living with his birth parents.

We learned that you have to meet the child where he is, and try to match the intensity. 'Wow, you're really showing me that you're upset!' would be said very loudly, and then we would keep talking, sometimes nonsense, slowly bringing our energy down to a calm state. Most of the time George would join in; sometimes not. On more than one occasion, if George was having a tantrum at home or in public(!), I would lie on the floor on my back and have a tantrum of my own, the picture of absurdity, which would then break George's concentration, and allow the regulation to happen. We had a very large and prevailing motto of not caring what anyone else thought at that point in time; I think that did more than anything else to get us through.

Much as we appreciated the support we got from our friends and family, there were certain things relating to behaviours, food and ways of parenting that they simply didn't and couldn't understand unless they had a connection to social work or psychology. It was hard not to be embarrassed when William's very proper, rather Victorian father choked on his tea as he watched George shovel endless food into his mouth, using his hands, and hitting the target only about 50 per cent of the time. You would think that if someone was using their hands to eat, they would at least get the food into their mouth! But no, hand–eye co-ordination was an issue for George, which meant (and, I have to say, still means) that using cutlery is a struggle.

Those early days were so similar to having an infant. We put a cloth down on the floor, and tried to put a bib around George's neck, just to minimise the mess. I despaired every time George came home from school; when he was in Year 1, I could still tell what the lunch had been by looking at his shirt. There was no re-wearing of uniforms, and an excessive amount of laundry. Eventually I gave in, and bought more uniforms so I didn't spend all my time washing and drying, or panicking in the morning.

Part of the problem with adopting a child who's lived their early life in adverse circumstances is that we're not mind-readers. As adoptive parents, we have to guess or assume where behaviours are coming from, and do our best to neutralise them. We have to think on our feet lightning-fast, and hope for the best. Not only were we re-wiring the part of George's brain that feared there wouldn't be enough food, but intrinsically linked to that was the belief that adults weren't to be trusted, that they didn't know what was best for him and that anything could disappear, so that he had to use whatever means available to him to get what he wanted.

We believe that relationships are paramount; your secure relationship with the child is more important than mundane things they should do. If brushing teeth is a massive struggle, just don't brush them this morning. It isn't worth the drama, if you haven't established a secure attachment – tooth brushing can come later!

I equate this model to many parents' experience of schooling under the coronavirus lockdown: eventually they realised that their relationship with their children was more important than battling over spellings or maths, so they learned to teach in an alternative and "off book" way: less academic, but far more peaceful!

In the early days, we did follow the approach set out in *Love Me, Feed Me*, as we trusted it as part of a larger plan. Predictably, George did gain weight for a time, but luckily, we have a dog and a scooter – a perfect excuse to exercise every day! We agreed with our therapy team to draw a line at giving George whatever he wanted to eat whenever he wanted it, particularly in relation to fatty or sugary food, but that meant some very creative thinking and planning ahead in case he saw that kind of food in the grocery store or when we were in the park.

One issue we faced was the fact that for the first two-and-a-half years of his life, when George had had to fend for himself, he would have eaten whatever he found... that's all well and good when you leave piles of carrot sticks and houmous, or apples and cheese around, but it is another thing entirely when you walk down the high street to go to the park in summertime! Following advice from our adoption agency, we would make sure to be the ones to suggest an ice cream long before we came to the ice cream stand – thus making the treat our idea; or we would make sure to go the long way round to avoid it entirely. When we are the ones suggesting something that George wants, it re-affirms the notion that we know what is best for him, and that doesn't always mean another carrot stick and houmous! If George saw something he wanted, and we said 'no', that's when the aggression and explosive tantrums would start. We had to think fast then, and either establish that treats were possible and our idea, so that it became a non-issue and hopefully averted a tantrum, or somehow distract him and remove ourselves from the situation.

We would also try to give any treats towards the beginning of exercise. However, it was a double-edged sword. On the one hand, George would work off the sugar rush before heading home, but on the other, it did increase the chances of him running off or not listening. Those days were all about damage control, thinking ahead, and trying to enjoy the positive moments as much as possible! And my goodness, were there lovely moments!

Over the course of really only a few weeks, George started regulating himself more and more. It was enough to know that any food left on his plate had been saved for him for later, and he wouldn't ask about it again. He stopped saying that he was hungry while he had his mouth full of food. As advised, we largely kept to ourselves for quite some time, while we got to know one another. When we ventured further afield, we'd ask friends to send a photograph of their full fridge before we went to visit them.

A couple of months into being a family, George's foster family came to visit us in the park for a picnic. It makes me laugh now, to think of their faces when I put a huge platter of wholewheat pasta with salmon flakes (along with peas and sweetcorn) into the centre of the blanket. I could see them glance at each other, thinking the same thing. If I were a mind reader, I imagine I would have heard something like 'Ha! What amateurs! Good luck, George is going to go crazy!' If they could have read our minds, it would have been something like 'Watch this!'

George ate one plate of pasta, asked for another, then left almost all of it on the plate, turned to his foster sister and said, 'Can we play now?'.

Yes, we felt slightly smug, but I think we'd earned our success!

This is not to say that we'd completely cracked it, or that it was easy, but it was certainly affirming to realise that our efforts were paying off, even in a situation that must have been stressful in spite of the happy reunion.

Due to the nature of our jobs, William and I decided that I should be the primary carer during the period between introductions and until the adoption was finalised. I worked as much as I could after George had gone to school or to bed, but during his home time, I was in charge and focused on him. I get bored by repetitive food, so always tried to invent new things to make for lunches and dinners. We spent hours baking together, kneading bread, measuring, trying not to spill anything, tasting dough. It was so good for both of us on so many levels.

Slowly, slowly

Ever since infancy, George had loved music; fascinatingly, we found that he would convey what he was feeling by becoming attached to certain songs and lyrics. "Help" by the Beatles was a favourite, particularly the line 'I need somebody, not just anybody'. We would dance around the kitchen, my son in my arms, covered in flour, or honey, or carrot peels. I'd spin him around (good for his equilibrium, not so good for my back) and sing the lyrics from the songs with him, over and over again. It was a magical time that I look back on with nostalgia... there's no way I could spin George around now! Throughout that time of linking food with joy, although I knew we were having fun, I also knew that we were doing invaluable re-learning as well as strengthening our attachment.

When William arrived home from work, George would proudly proclaim that we'd made bread or "nanna cakes" (banana bread muffins – before they were fashionable, I might add!). Or sometimes it was a homemade chicken pie, or pizza. We were instilling in him the idea that food is something you make, perhaps grow, that you know what's in it, and how it is prepared, so that you can enjoy it. More than once, an entire plate of "nanna cakes" would magically disappear when I went to the loo or made a phone call. Luckily, as I knew we'd made them with coconut sugar and wholewheat flour, I'd make some casual remark about saving some for Pops, but actually I appreciated the cheekiness, and above all else, that George was aware that he wouldn't be punished for eating if that's what he really had to do.

Our first Hallowe'en together was a real learning experience! We were like "wooden toys only" parents at Legoland! There was very little we could do about the sugar and chocolate intake. Our itsy bitsy spider George (cute costume) was basically a kid in a candy shop at our neighbour's Hallowe'en party. We did as many parents attempt to do, and suggested a limit on the sweets, which was observed while he remained in our eye line. Unbeknown to us, of course, George was actually stuffing his face with chocolates when he was out of the room. Interestingly, more than half a year since becoming a family, when we got home, George threw up from eating too much. He learned a valuable lesson that day, one he reminds us of even now: it's possible to overeat, and the body has a way of dealing with that; it no longer needed to worry as much about starving and saving up as many calories as possible, and could become more discriminating about what it ate. Another (gross) success.

As part of our game plan, no matter what we were doing, or where we were going, we always made sure to have snacks on us. Our training had taught us that a protein-rich meal does a similar thing to the brain as the hormone cortisol in helping to self-soothe, whereas sugar has the opposite effect. We found that apples on their own would make George's body feel that he was eating something, but then we'd have a sugar rush to deal with, so we made sure to have Babybel mini-cheeses, or cheese sticks alongside.

Planning, prevention and damage control. That was the mantra when it came to food and behaviours!

I did everything in my power to avoid situations that I knew had the potential to be volatile. I made sure to do the grocery shopping when I was on my own, and was always on high alert for potential dramas if we were out and about. If we went to the zoo, I'd suggest a treat right away, or pull out a high-protein snack just before arriving. Any transition was stressful for George, and his go-to mode of coping was to think that he must be hungry and needed to eat. Our prevention method wasn't always successful, of course. I vividly remember one incident when we had no choice but to take George into the grocery store, and when I said, 'Let's have this instead of that', he head-butted me so hard in the jaw I saw stars, and tears came to my eyes. I believe we left right away without getting anything...but no one's perfect and it was me that needed regulating!

To add to our seemingly fussy ideas about ingredients: George's social work team and doctors had believed that cow's milk gave George a bloated stomach. All through nursery, we kept their fridge and ours stocked with milk alternatives. It was only after half a year in reception class, during one of the millions of meetings we were required to attend, that the teachers mentioned how much milk George drank at lunch. 'Wait', we said, 'You mean soya milk?'; 'Oh no, he's been drinking regular milk all year'.

Well. Best laid plans.

Now George consumes vast quantities of milk. His teeth and bones are very healthy, and he's grown nearly two feet since we brought him home. I suppose I'll concede that he is listening to his body...although we've had very few experiences of his body telling him that enough was enough already, on the milk front.

Slowly, slowly, with our mealtimes primarily at home where portions were large and relatively healthy, the conversations wouldn't always veer back to food. We found we had a mutual love of dinosaurs, which became a great and ongoing bond.

Stressful situations would trigger George's fear of not having enough. Although this has decreased dramatically over the years, it is still true. We went to William's sister's home to celebrate our first Christmas together, six months after George came to us. We had a fabulous time, with all the trimmings: singing, dancing, eating. Bedtime, however, was hilarious. As William was putting George into his pyjamas, I pulled back the sheets to realise that he'd been stockpiling cookies and a myriad of sweets in his bed. His trouser pockets were full to bursting with half-melted chocolate buttons.

Shortly after that, seven months on from becoming a family, we flew to Disney World for my sister's wedding. A volume could be written about how difficult it was to walk around Disney World with a sensory-seeking child who has behavioural difficulties and a tendency to run off, but the funniest moment occurred, as it often does, in a pub. We had gone out to eat with my American grandparents to an Irish pub...in Florida. Again, George's eating habits drew astonished looks from relatives. Somehow, before we knew it, the Irish dancing troop onstage asked for volunteers to learn a few steps, and being the excellent dancer he is, George ran up to the stage. Before our very eyes, he was learning a bit of Irish step dancing. I wonder if anyone else noticed the globs of mashed potatoes falling out of his pockets as he bounced up and down to the sounds of a tin flute?

Reflections: from four years until today

There isn't much to say, or that stands out, about what's happened between then and now. Gradually, George's fear of not having enough food faded away. We reached another milestone when he started turning down food for being too spicy, or simply not liking it. Although it meant that we had to avoid certain foods and be more aware of ingredients and flavours, it actually meant that George felt safe enough to refuse food, trusting that we'd give him something else.

Within a year, we'd forget to carry snacks on us without causing an international incident. By this time, we wouldn't have to show George photos of our friends' fridges before visiting, nor make excuses in advance for his quirky relationship with food. Within two years, we all stopped talking about food in the same desperate way, and more as a family with secure attachments. As the effects of sugar have become less apparent (whether that's due to George's maturation or something psychological, I don't know), we've become more relaxed about what we eat for pudding or the occasional snack.

Looking back, I suppose that there was a direct correlation between George's increasing attachment to us and a decreased fear about food. It really was psychological as much as physical.

As I write this, it is more than four years since we brought George home to live with us. Last week, at eight years old, he started back to school after the overlong summer break due to Covid-19. Considering the virus, a new teacher in a new classroom and attempts at social distancing, it's no wonder that some of the old fears and insecurities resurfaced. Frankly, I was anxious as well! The first two evenings after school, I found the grapes I'd packed him for a snack still in his pockets, showing us that somewhere inside he still had the urge to hoard food in case he needed it (I learned the hard way that environmentally-friendly paper snack bags may not be ideal). However, George is using cutlery more and more, with frequent reminders, and he's able to wear school sweatshirts and shorts a second time, as they less frequently look like a Jackson Pollock painting by the time he gets home.

Understanding that George's food worries were based on real-life experiences and legitimate fears has given us infinite patience. I firmly believe that addressing the root of the problem in a drastic and alternative way, rather than putting a plaster on the symptom and hoping for the best, is how we've got to the point of it no longer being a real issue. We had to be patient and trusting with ourselves as well as George, and develop a thick skin regarding what other people thought about our methods. After all, it's what we needed to do for our son; he is happy, and healthy, and that's all we ever wanted.

Authors' comments

This beautifully honest account by one of George's adoptive parents illustrates several key points. Firstly, how important it is for adoptive parents to have the active support of an agency in tackling food issues from the therapeutic perspective of trauma and attachment. What the parent's account also conveys is how well George's adoptive parents contextualised his eating difficulties in relation to his early life history, which enabled them to be empathetic and thoughtful in their response. There are delightful vignettes in this account of a creative parenting approach and the adoration and love from George's parents shines through. Inevitably, mistakes are made on this journey with food, but what the adoptive parents highlight is that mistakes can be repaired.

Early intervention prevented eating difficulties becoming entrenched and a battleground, which would no doubt have exacerbated some of the other problems George was struggling with in his new family. Due to the holistic approach, the interconnection between food, trauma and attachment were understood and eating difficulties were treated as an integral part of overall development recovery. What this case example also highlights is how complex food, nutrition and eating skills are, involving sensory processing, the stress hormone system and the attachment relationship dynamic. It is wonderful that George and his adoptive parents are now on such a positive trajectory, which they might not have been if food and eating had not been addressed early on.

References

Ayres AJ (1972) 'Types of sensory integrative dysfunction among disabled learners', *American Journal of Occupational Therapy*, 26, pp. 13–18

Bernston GG and Tsakiris M (2019) 'Interoception and the autonomic nervous system: bottom up meets top down', in Tsakiris M and De Preester H (eds), *The Interoceptive Basis of the Mind*, pp. 3–23, Oxford: Oxford University Press

Birch L, Savage J and Ventura A (2007) 'Influences on the development of children's eating behaviours: from infancy to adolescence', *Canadian Journal of Dietetic Practice and Research*, 68:1, S1–S56

Caroline Walker Trust (2001) *Eating Well for Looked After Children and Young People, Nutritional and Practical*

Guidelines: Report of an expert working group, London: Caroline Walker Trust

Cohn A (2006) *Constipation, Withholding and your Child*, London: Jessica Kingsley Publishers

Cox R, Skouteris H, Hemmingsson E, Fuller-Tyszkiewicz M and Hardy L (2016) 'Problematic eating and food-related behaviours and excessive weight gain: why children in out-of-home care are at risk', *Australian Social Work* online journal, 69:3, pp. 338–47

Flatters I, Mushtaq F, Hill LJ, Holt RJ, Wilkie RM and Mon-Williams M (2014) 'The relationship between experimental brain research and child's postural stability and manual dexterity', *Experimental Brain Research*, 232:9, pp. 2907–2917

Gajos JM and Beaver KM (2016) 'The effect of Omega 3 fatty acids on aggression: a meta analysis', *Neuro Science and Biobehavioral Reviews*, 69, pp. 147–58

Herbert BM and Pollatos O (2019) 'The relevance of interoception for eating and eating disorders', in Tsakiris M and De Preester H (eds), *The Interoceptive Basis of the Mind*, Oxford: Oxford University Press, pp. 165–187

Hughes D (2013) *Parenting a Child with Emotional and Behavioural Difficulties*, London: CoramBAAF

Hui Y (2013) 'Feeding behaviour of infants and young children and its impact on child psychosocial and emotional development', in *Encyclopedia on Early Childhood Development*, University of San Diego, available online at: www.child-encyclopedia.com/child-nutrition/

according-experts/feeding-behaviour-infants-and-young-children-and-its-impact-child

Khalsa S et al (2018) 'Interception and mental health: a roadmap', *Biological Psychiatry: Cognitive neuroscience and neuroimaging*, 3:6, pp. 50–13

Kutter A, Hanesch C, Rauh C and Delgado A (2011) 'Impact of proprioception and tactile sensations in the mouth on the perceived thickness of semi-solid foods', *Food Quality and Preference*, 22, pp. 193–197

Larkin H, Felitti VJ and Anda RF (2014) 'Social work and adverse childhood experiences research: implications for practice and health policy', *Social Work in Public Health*, 29:1, pp. 1–16

Lau C (2015) 'Development of suck and swallow mechanisms in infants', *Annals of Nutrition & Metabolism*, 66 Suppl 5 (05), pp. 7–14

Le Révérend BJ, Edelson LR and Loret C (2014) 'Anatomical, functional, physiological and behavioural aspects of the development of mastication in early childhood', *British Journal of Nutrition*, 111:3, pp. 403–14

Linscott D and Lim J (2016) 'Retronasal odor enhancement by salty and unami tastes', *Food Quality and Preference*, 48, pp. 1–10

Martin IE, Dourish CT, Rotshtein P, Spetter MS and Higgs S (2019) 'Interoception and disorder eating: a systematic review', *Neuroscience & Biobehavioral Reviews*, 107, pp. 166–191

Matsuo K and Palmer JB (2008) 'Anatomy and physiology of feeding and swallowing: normal and abnormal', *Physical Medicine and Rehabilitation Clinics of North America*, 19:4, pp. 691–707

May-Benson TA and Goodrich L (2018) *The Focus Program for Mealtime Success Manual*, Newton, MA: Spiral Foundation

McCullough E, Gordon Jones S, Last A, Vaughan A and Burnell J (2016) 'An evaluation of Neuro-Physiological Psychotherapy: an integrative approach to working with children who have experienced early life trauma', *Clinical Child Psychology & Psychiatry*, 21:4, pp. 582–602

McCullough E and Mathura A (2019) 'Control group evaluation of Neuro-Physiological Psychotherapy (NPP)', *Child Abuse & Neglect*, 97, pp. 104–128

Oldroyd K, Pasupathi M and Wainryb C (2019) 'Social antecedents to the development of interoception: attachment related processes are associated with interoception', *Frontiers in Psychology*, 10, p. 712

Post B (2009) *The Great Behaviour Breakdown*, Palmyra, VA: Post Institutes

Prescott J (2015) 'Multisensory processes in flavour perception and their influence on food choice', *Current Opinion in Food Science*, 3, pp. 47–52

Przybylka M (2016) *Care for Something to Eat?*, available online at: www.foodincare.org.uk

Rowell K (2012) *Love Me, Feed Me: The adoptive parent's guide to ending the worry about weight*, Saint Paul, MN: Family Feeding Dynamic

Savaglio M, Bergmeier H, Green R, O'Donnell R, Pizzirani B, Bruce L and Skouteris H (2019) 'Problematic eating interventions in out-of-home care: the need for a trauma-informed, attachment-focused approach', *Australian Social Work*, 69, pp. 338–347

Spence C (2015) 'Multisensory flavor perception', *Cell*, 161:1, pp. 24–35

Tsakiris M (2017) 'The multi-sensory basis of the self: from body to identity to others', *Quarterly Journal of Experimental Psychology*, 70:4, pp. 597–609

Twatchman-Reilly J, Amaral SC and Zebrowski PP (2008) 'Addressing feeding disorders in children on the autistic spectrum in school-based settings: physiological and behavioral issues', *Language, Speech and Hearing Services in Schools*, 39:2, pp. 261–72

Van der Kolk (2014) *The Body Keeps the Score: Brain, mind and body in the healing of trauma*, London: Penguin

Vaughan J, Burnell A and McCullough (2016) 'Neuro-Physiological Psychotherapy (NPP): the development and application of an integrative wrap around service and treatment programme for maltreated children placed in adoptive and foster care placements', *Journal of Clinical Child Psychology & Psychiatry*: 21:4, pp. 568–81

Wade TJ, Bowden J and Sites HJ (2018) 'Child maltreatment and motor co-ordination deficits amongst preschool children', *Journal of Child & Adolescent Trauma*, 11:2, pp. 159–62

Wilbarger J, Gunnar M, Schneideer M and Pollak S (2010) 'Sensory processing and internationally adopted, post-institutionalised children', *Journal of Child Psychology and Psychiatry and Allied Disciplines*, 51:10, pp. 1105–1114

Glossary

Attention Deficit Hyperactivity Disorder (ADHD)
Attention Deficit Hyperactivity Disorder (ADHD) is a condition that affects children's behaviour. Children with ADHD can seem restless, may have trouble concentrating and may act on impulse. Symptoms of ADHD tend to be noticed at an early age and may become more noticeable when a child's circumstances change, such as when they start school. Most cases are diagnosed when children are 6–12 years old. The symptoms of ADHD usually improve with age, but many adults who were diagnosed with the condition at a young age continue to experience problems. People with ADHD may also have additional problems, such as sleep and anxiety disorders.

Autism Spectrum Disorder (ASD)
Autism Spectrum Disorder (ASD) is a developmental disorder that affects communication and behaviour. Although autism can be

diagnosed at any age, it is said to be a "developmental disorder" because symptoms generally appear in the first two years of life. Children with ASD have:

- difficulty with communication and interaction with other people;
- restricted interests and repetitive behaviours;
- symptoms that impair the child's ability to function properly in school and other areas of life.

Autism is known as a "spectrum" disorder because there is wide variation in the type and severity of symptoms people experience. Autism occurs in all ethnic, racial, and economic groups. Although ASD can be a lifelong disorder, treatments and services can improve a person's symptoms and ability to function.

Cortisol
Cortisol is a steroid hormone that regulates a wide range of processes throughout the body, including metabolism and the immune response. It also has a very important role in helping the body respond to stress.

Developmental trauma
Developmental trauma is not a formal diagnosis, but is terminology that is now generally accepted as the best way of describing the developmental impact of trauma on a child's development.

Dyadic Developmental Psychotherapy (DDP)
Dyadic Developmental Psychotherapy (DDP) is a dyadic therapy, parenting approach and model for practice that uses what we know about attachment and developmental trauma to help children and families with their relationships.

Extraceptive information

Extraceptive information is information that we all gather from the environment around us through our senses.

Foetal Alcohol Spectrum Disorder (FASD)

Foetal Alcohol Spectrum Disorder (FASD) is a term used to describe the impact on the brain and body of individuals prenatally exposed to alcohol during pregnancy (i.e. when a baby is in the womb). FASD is a lifelong disability. Individuals with FASD have their own unique areas of difficulties and may experience challenges in their daily living and need support with motor skills, physical health, learning, memory, attention, emotional regulation and social skills. They also have a unique set of strengths and many show talents that, when nurtured and supported, demonstrate their unlimited potential in those areas. FASD is an umbrella term for several diagnoses that are all related to prenatal exposure to alcohol. These are:

- Foetal Alcohol Syndrome (FAS);
- Partial Foetal Alcohol Syndrome (PFAS);
- Alcohol Related Neuro-developmental Disorder (ARND);
- Alcohol Related Birth Defects (ARBD).

Interoceptive information

Interoceptive information is information that we all gather through our senses about our internal physiological state and body functions.

Motor skills

Motor skills are movements and actions of the bone structures. Typically, they are categorised into two groups: gross motor skills and fine motor skills. Gross motor skills are involved in movement and co-ordination of the arms, legs, and other large body parts. Fine motor skills are movements involving smaller muscle groups such as those in the hand and wrist.

Neuro-physiological psychotherapy (NPP)
Neuro-physiological psychotherapy (NPP) is a dyadic therapy for children who are traumatised and have attachment difficulties. It integrates a range of different disciplines and therapeutic approaches to provide an integrative wrap-around therapy. It also works with the family as a whole and their wider network.

Neuroscience
Neuroscience refers to a body of knowledge that has grown rapidly in the last 25 years, that relates to research and theories about the brain and the central nervous system and their functioning.

Neuro-sequential
Neuro-sequential describes a therapeutic approach that follows the development of the brain and nervous system from the primitive brain, to the mid (limbic) brain, to the higher cortical brain (cortex). This approach moves from a regulatory focus, to an attachment relationship focus, to problem-solving and reflective capacity.

Sensory integration assessment
Sensory integration is a term used to describe processes in the brain that allow us to take information we receive from our senses, organise it, and respond appropriately.

An occupational therapist (OT) trained in sensory integration to a minimum of Level 4/M6 would help you identify whether your child has sensory integration or sensory processing difficulties that may be impacting their well-being and stopping them reaching their physical potential.

Sensory motor development

Sensory motor development is the process whereby a child gains use and co-ordination of their muscles of the trunk, arms, legs and hands (motor development), and begins to experience (through sensory input) the environment through sight, sounds, smell, taste and hearing.

Sensory Processing Disorder or difficulties (SPD)

Sensory processing issues are difficulties with organising and responding to information that comes in through the senses. Children may be over-sensitive to sensory input, under-sensitive, or both.

Somatosensory

The somatosensory system is a part of the sensory nervous system. The somatosensory system is a complex system of sensory neurons and neural pathways that responds to changes at the surface or inside the body.

Useful organisations

British Nutrition Foundation
Information about healthy eating with special reference to children.
www.nutrition.org.uk/healthyliving/lifestages/children.html

Chrysalis Associates
A therapeutic team of professionals drawn from the fields of social work, clinical and educational psychology, who specialise in the assessment and treatment of developmental trauma and attachment difficulties.
48 Wostenholme Road
Nether Edge
Sheffield S7 1LL
Tel: 0144 2509 455
www.chrysalisassociates.org

Family Futures
A voluntary adoption agency and independent fostering provider, as well as an assessment and treatment service for traumatised children.
3 & 4 Floral Place
7–9 Southampton Grove
London N1 2PL
Tel: 020 7354 4161
www.familyfutures.co.uk

NHS Eat Well Guide
An interactive guide to show how much of what we eat should come from each food group to achieve a healthy, balanced diet.
www.nhs.uk/live-well/eat-well/the-eatwell-guide/

PAC – UK (part of Family Action)
A post-adoption support agency that offers a range of support and counselling to adopted children, families, and adopted adults.
34 Wharf Road
London N1 7GR
Tel: 020 7284 0555
Advice line: 0113 230 210
www.pac-uk.org/

The Anna Freud Centre
An organisation that provides services to families and children with emotional, behavioural and developmental difficulties.
12 Maresfield Gardens
London NW3 5SU
Tel: 020 7794 2313
www.annafreud.org

PARENTING MATTERS

This unique series provides expert knowledge about a range of children's health conditions, coupled with facts, figures and guidance presented in a straightforward and accessible style. Adopters and foster carers also describe what it is like to parent an affected child, "telling it like it is", sharing their parenting experiences and offering useful advice.

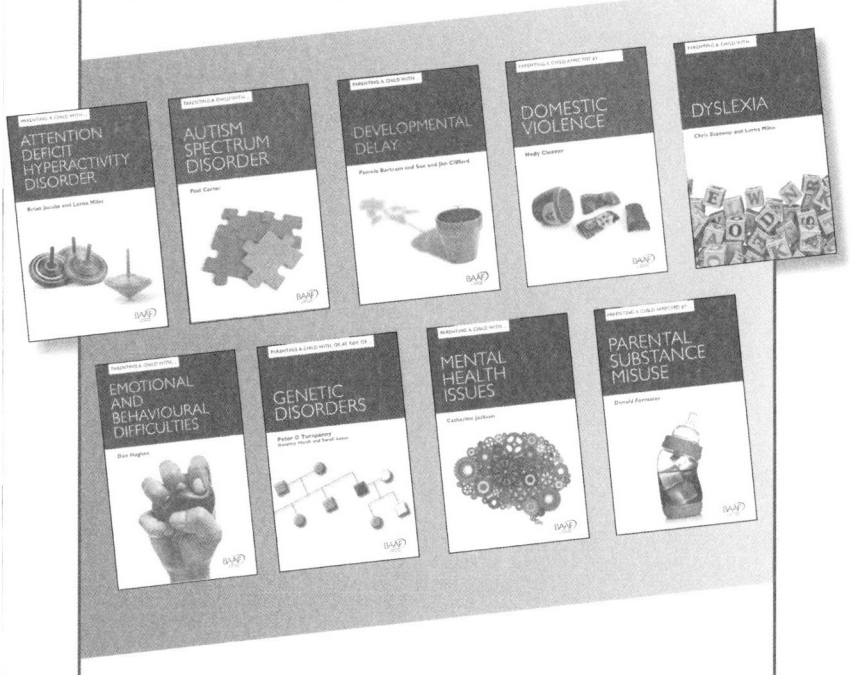

To find out more visit **www.corambaaf.org.uk/bookshop**